gourmet

THAI

in minutes

gourmet
THAI
in minutes

over 120 inspirational recipes

vatcharin
bhumichitr

Photography by Martin Brigdale
and Somchai Phongphaisarnkit

Kyle Books

For David Sweetman

This edition published in 2007 by Kyle Books
An imprint of Kyle Cathie Limited
www.kylecathie.com

Distributed by National Book Network
4501 Forbes Boulevard, Suite 200
Lanham, MD 20706
Phone (301) 459 3366

Text © 2004 Vatcharin Bhumichitr
Food photography © 2004 Martin Brigdale
Travel photography © 2004 Somchai Phongphaisarnkit
Book design © 2004 Kyle Cathie Limited

ISBN 978-1-904920-74-8

Library of Congress Cataloging-in-Publication data available upon request.

1 2 3 4 5 08 07 06 05 04

Senior Editor: Muna Reyal
Designer: Geoff Hayes
Photographer: Martin Brigdale
Home Economist: Sunil Vijayakar
Styling: Helen Trent
Copy Editor: Ruth Baldwin
Editorial Assistant: Jennifer Wheatley
Production: Sha Huxtable and Alice Holloway

Color reproduction by Sang Choy
Printed and bound in Singapore by Star Standard

contents

introduction

In Thailand, food and entertainment are inseparable. Eating is always considered to be more fun (*sanuk*) in a group, and the larger the better. We love parties. Whether for a young boy about to become a monk, a harvest festival, a wedding, or even a funeral, food and entertainment are always called for and enthusiastically provided. Indeed, the rhythmic sounds of cooking, the chopping of meats, the crushing of herbs, the pestle beating in the mortar, and the rattle of cooking pans used to be carefully listened to by the single men of the community—a good rhythm being indicative of a good cook and therefore a good wife.

Food and Culture

When the Thai food festival was set up ten years ago at London's Battersea Park to promote Thai food, we soon realized that this important ingredient—entertainment—was missing. So I arranged for a stage to be created and invited performers to show the different types of entertainment from Thailand, including Thai classical dance, folk opera (*Likay*), and folk music (*Luk Thoong*). Demonstrations of fruit carving and stalls selling crafts and goods for the home completed the festive atmosphere. The inspiration for this came from the Thai Temple Fair (*Ngarn Wat*), where the local temple holds a festival, normally for a few days, with music, dancing, food, and stands selling all kinds of goods, clothes, toys, and household utensils. These festivals are always well attended by local people, who see them as a good opportunity to go out and have a good time, but they also benefit the community by providing money for the local temples, which are still very central to life in Thailand.

In this book I have tried to blend the food and entertainment of Thailand to give you a taste of our culture and to show you how our entertainment, like our cooking, has evolved into a fusion of the old and the new, traditional and stylish. For Thai people, food and entertainment are always enjoyed together, and I have been passionate about them both since I was a child. I would like to share this love with you and so I have begun each chapter with a brief introduction to the various types of entertainment that we enjoy with our food.

I have enjoyed doing the research for this book and hope it will help you to appreciate and understand Thai food and culture.

ingredients

Bean Curd

Bean curd, or tofu, is made from the liquid extracted from yellow soybeans. It is available at most supermarkets. The liquid it comes in should be discarded before cooking. Bean curd is delicate and it is best to use it as soon as possible after purchase. In some places it can be bought prepared.

Holy Basil

Holy basil is generally available either fresh or dried in Asian markets. It has a stronger, more intense taste than sweet basil and has to be cooked to release its flavor. If it is not available, sweet basil can be used instead.

Chilies

The chilies I use are generally available from Asian markets. The smallest are the hottest. The amounts suggested in the recipes will give a taste that Thais would consider okay, but not really hot. You will have to experiment a little to find the level of heat that you like. To reduce the heat, use fewer chilies or seed them and remove the membranes, which will lessen the heat but keep the flavor. Be careful, after cutting or chopping chilies, to wash your hands thoroughly before touching any sensitive areas of your body, such as your eyes and face.

Coconut

Coconut is an essential ingredient in Thai cooking. The coconut palm also produces wood for housing and utensils, leaves for roofing and matting, and gourds for holding food and drink—a useful tree indeed! Fresh coconuts are available at certain times of the year in Asian markets. The liquid you hear sloshing around inside is coconut juice, not milk, and makes a refreshing drink. Coconut milk and cream are both made from the grated flesh of the coconut, to which warm water is added and the mixture repeatedly squeezed until it becomes cloudy. When this mixture is strained, it is coconut milk; if this is left to stand, coconut cream will float to the surface in much the same way as cream does on regular milk. Coconut milk is now widely available in cartons and cans, and even in Thailand many people use canned milk for convenience and speed.

Cilantro

Cilantro, also known as coriander leaves or Chinese parsley, is a green herb much used as a garnish in Thai cooking, either whole or chopped. It is generally available in bunches or as a growing herb in a pot from supermarkets and Asian markets. Coriander root is also much used in Thai cooking, but if you cannot get ahold of it, just use an extra length of the lower part of the stalk.

Eggplants

I use several different types of eggplant here. The Thai eggplant commonly available in Asian markets is round, pale green, and about an inch in diameter. Do not confuse it with the smaller Thai pea eggplant (generally rarer outside Thailand), which is more bitter.

Galangal

This is a type of ginger with a more translucent, pink tinge. It is peeled, then thinly sliced for ease of cooking. It is generally available in Asian markets.

Krachai

Another type of ginger, but with thin and relatively straight roots, and with a fiercer taste than galangal. It is sometimes available in Asian markets, but can also be bought dried.

Lemongrass

Another indispensable ingredient of Thai cuisine. The stalks are bought in bundles of six to eight, and are usually about eight to ten inches long. Trim the ends and finely slice the stalks. When bought, they do not smell, but when you crush them, they give off a refreshing lemon aroma.

Lime Leaves

These are the dark green leaves of the Kaffir lime and impart a pungent lemon-lime flavor. The easiest way to slice them is with kitchen scissors.

Tamarind Water

You can buy the pulp of the tamarind fruit in packages. To extract the juice or water, dissolve the pulp in hot water, then strain the mixture. If tamarind water is not available, use lemon juice, but double the stated quantity.

Broth

Many of the recipes call for broth, and I appreciate that making and keeping broth may not be practical for many people. In some recipes, water can be used; in others, you will have to use bouillon cubes. However, if you have the time to make broth, this is how I do it.

For meat broth, simply cover some meat bones with water, bring to a boil, and simmer for at least two hours, skimming the scum off the surface from time to time. Do not use any herbs or spices. Add more bones as needed, and remember that you must boil the broth every day before using or keep it frozen.

For vegetable broth, you will need one onion, quartered; two carrots, roughly chopped; two celery stalks, roughly chopped; three or four coriander (cilantro) roots; and one teaspoon black peppercorns. Most hard vegetables will do, but avoid highly colored ones such as beets. Cover with water and bring to a boil. Continue boiling until the liquid is reduced by about a fifth.

Oil

I do not specify any type of cooking oil, and almost any will do except olive oil, which has too pronounced a flavor for Thai food.

Sauces

Bean Sauce *(Tow Jiew)*

Bean sauce is made from slightly mashed, fermented soybeans, either black or yellow. It helps to thicken a dish as well as add flavor. Black bean sauce is thick and deeply colored, and is used to give a richer flavor than can be achieved with dark soy sauce. Yellow bean sauce is more salty and pungent, but again it is a quite subtle refinement. If you rarely cook Asian food, a jar of black bean sauce will suffice. Nowadays you can buy small jars of both types, which should keep almost indefinitely if refrigerated.

Fish Sauce *(Nam Pla)*

This is the main flavoring for Thai cooking, for which there is no substitute. It is the salt of Southeast Asia. Although it can be made from shrimp, it is most commonly extracted from salted, fermented fish. The best is homemade and has a light whiskey color and a refreshing, salty taste, rather than being dark with a heavy, bitter tang and a powerful, fishy aroma. When buying commercially produced fish sauce, I try to find a lighter, rather than darker, liquid. Color can also indicate if a bottle has been open too long, as the sauce darkens with age. If it has noticeably changed color, it should be discarded.

Oyster Sauce *(Nam Man Hoy)*

This sauce is also of Chinese origin. It is made from oysters that have been cooked in soy sauce and then mixed with seasonings and brine. The result, however, tastes of fish, as might be expected. It should be stored in a refrigerator.

Soy Sauce *(Siew)*

Chinese in origin, soy sauce is made from salted, cooked soybeans fermented with flour, after which the liquid is extracted. There are two varieties available commercially: light soy sauce, which is thin, with a clear, delicate flavor, mild enough to be used as a condiment; and dark soy sauce, which is thicker, with a stronger, sweeter flavor, having been fermented with other ingredients such as mushrooms and ginger, that darken the final liquid. The difference between the light and dark is slight, the dark being used to color food. If you rarely cook Asian food, a bottle of light soy sauce will suffice.

Techniques

With Thai food, the time spent actually cooking is quite short, making it ideal for a dinner party, but you do need to have everything prepared beforehand.

Vegetables such as chilies, ginger, shallots, and garlic should be finely sliced or even smashed using the side of a Chinese cleaver. Hard vegetables like carrots and potatoes should be cut into small pieces; green vegetables such as broccoli should be in small florets. Meat should be either ground or sliced into bite-size pieces.

Nearly every recipe has the instruction "stir-fry" somewhere in it. As the term implies, the ingredients are stirred while cooking. Simple and fast, stir-frying is best done in a long-handled wok over a high heat. The idea of cooking quickly is to seal in the flavors. Vegetables should be cooked for the minimum amount of time and remain crisp and bright. Do not overcook.

The Thai Meal

The ideal Thai meal consists of a number of small dishes shared by a group of friends or family. Rice is ladled onto each plate and everybody takes a little of each dish to eat with the rice—you would never take a large serving. Sharing is essential. Most of the recipes in this book are suitable for a meal for four people sharing dishes. A typical meal would consist of two or three appetizers, plus one salad dish brought out before the main meal and served with drinks. Rice would then be served with a soup, a curry, and two main dishes, followed by fruit or a dessert. The Thai use spoons and forks, only using chopsticks for noodles.

appetizers
& snacks

classical dance

The Thai dramatic arts, such as the *Khon* mask dance (pictured at right) and the *Lakhon* style of Thai classical dance (pictured on the previous pages), are based on Thai literature.

The Khon style of dance performance is characterized by energetic and highly stylized action. The Khon dancers begin their training when very young, and will often join Thailand's National Dance and Music College in Bangkok around the age of ten.

In a Khon performance, acting and dancing are inseparable. Each gesture in the play is significant and conveys a meaning. The action of the moment, such as walking, marching, or laughing, is reflected in the pace and character of the background music, which is performed by an orchestra of classical instruments. Singers offstage perform the narratives and the songs of individual dancers. Usually it is the men who wear the masks onstage, while the women have high, gilded crowns or headdresses.

The Lakhon style of dance drama is much less formal than the Khon style, and the actors do not normally wear masks, unless in the role of monkeys or other nonhuman or celestial beings. Lakhon plots are mainly drawn from traditional folk stories such as the *Ramakian, Jakatas,* and similar folk tales. While Khon and Lakhon costumes are basically the same, the Lakhon dance movements are much more graceful and sensual, with the upper body and hands being used expressively to convey specific emotions.

There are variations of Lakhon dance, the main one being *Lakhon Chatri*—the simplest in form and presentation. At Luk Muang, Bangkok's city pillar shrine, you can see the Lakhon Chatri performed at the request of supplicants thanking the deity for wishes granted.

The more stylized and graceful *Lakhon Nai* dance was primarily seen among the court ladies at the palace. Men, however, monopolized the *Lakhon Nok* plays, which were seen outside the palace and consisted of lively music, humor, and rapid, animated movements.

Traditional Thai dance is embedded in the ancient culture of my beautiful land. Of course, these days Thai youths are as influenced as all others around the world by the modern trends in popular music, but it is my hope that enough of each new generation will want to invest their time, energy, and commitment to continuing the traditional dance culture to preserve this ancient heritage for all to enjoy.

I have chosen classical dance to open this chapter, as the presentation of appetizers and snacks is often as elaborate as the staging of these performances. I hope that you will be tempted to try the recipes, and if in Thailand, to go and see some dance performances.

spring rolls
po pia tod

6 large spring roll wrappers, quartered

1 tablespoon cornstarch, mixed with a little water to make a paste

Oil, for deep-frying

For the filling

4 ounces soaked wun sen noodles (cellophane noodles), chopped
(1½ cups)

2 ounces presoaked dried wood ear mushrooms, chopped (1 cup)

1 cup bean sprouts

2 ounces carrots, finely diced (about ½ cup)

1 teaspoon finely chopped garlic

1 teaspoon light soy sauce

½ teaspoon ground white pepper

For the sweet chili sauce

6 tablespoons rice vinegar

¼ cup sugar

½ teaspoon salt

3 small fresh red or green chilies, finely chopped

Place all the filling ingredients in a mixing bowl and stir well. Set aside.
Heat the vinegar and stir in the sugar until dissolved. Stir in the salt
and chilies. Scoop into a bowl and set aside. Stir just before serving.

Place a little filling on each quartered wrapper. Fold in two opposite
corners, then roll across to form a plump roll. Use a little cornstarch
paste to seal. Heat the oil and fry the rolls until golden brown, drain
on paper towels, and serve with the sweet chili sauce and salad leaves.

Preparation time: 15 minutes   Cooking time: 5 minutes

shrimp and lychee
spring rolls
po pia kung

12 spring roll or egg roll sheets, each 1 inches square

6 large raw shrimp, peeled but with the tail left on, deveined, and
cut in half lengthwise

6 large lychees (fresh or canned), peeled and roughly chopped

Salt and ground black pepper

1 egg, beaten

Oil, for deep-frying

Sweet chili sauce (see recipe at left), for serving

Take one spring roll wrapper and fold over one corner toward the
center. Lay a shrimp half on the wrapper, its tail hanging over the
folded edge. Lay half of one chopped lychee along the length of
the shrimp and sprinkle with salt and pepper. Roll up the wrapper
over the shrimp so that you are left with a cylinder with the tail
protruding from one end. Seal the spring roll with beaten egg.
Repeat the process to make the remaining spring rolls. Set aside.

Heat a pan of oil for deep-frying to 400°F. Deep-fry the spring rolls
until they are golden brown all over. Drain on paper towels and serve
hot with the sweet chili sauce.

Preparation time: 10 minutes   Cooking time: 5 minutes

steamed stuffed wontons

kanom jeep

2 eggs

15 whole black peppercorns

2 cilantro roots, roughly chopped

2 tablespoons oil

2 small garlic cloves, finely chopped

4 ounces bamboo shoots, finely chopped (about $^{3}/_{4}$ cup)

4 ounces water chestnuts, finely chopped (about $^{3}/_{4}$–1 cup)

1 large onion, finely chopped

2 teaspoons all-purpose flour

2 tablespoons light soy sauce

1 teaspoon sugar

20 wonton wrappers

Lettuce and cilantro leaves, to garnish

For the sour soy sauce

3 tablespoons light soy sauce

1 tablespoon white vinegar

1 teaspoon sugar

3 small fresh red or green chilies, finely chopped

Hard-boil the eggs, chop finely, and set aside.

In a mortar, pound the peppercorns and cilantro roots until a paste forms, then set aside.

In a wok or frying pan, heat the oil, fry the garlic until golden brown, and set aside with the oil.

In a bowl, mix the bamboo shoots, water chestnuts, onion, the pepper and cilantro root paste, flour, soy sauce, sugar, and chopped eggs, stirring well until a firm mixture is formed.

Separate the wonton wrappers. Place a nugget of filling at the center of each wrapper. Gather up the edges of the wrapper and crimp together to form a tiny cup. Arrange the cups in a steamer and steam for 15 minutes.

Meanwhile, make the sour soy sauce by stirring all the ingredients together in a small bowl.

Just before serving, drip a little of the reserved garlic oil onto each wonton cup, garnish with the lettuce and cilantro leaves, and serve with the sour soy sauce.

Preparation time: 15 minutes   Cooking time: 15 minutes

vegetable wontons

geo tod

20 wonton wrappers

Oil, for deep-frying, plus 1 tablespoon

For the filling

2 teaspoons garlic, roughly chopped

1 teaspoon whole black peppercorns

$^1/_2$ cup finely chopped potato

$^2/_3$ cup finely chopped onion

$^2/_3$ cup finely chopped carrots

$^1/_2$ cup boiled corn kernels

$^1/_2$ teaspoon salt

1 tablespoon curry powder

1 tablespoon light soy sauce

1 teaspoon sugar

Sweet chili sauce (see page 17)

To make the filling, pound together the garlic and peppercorns in a mortar to form a paste. Heat one tablespoon of oil, briefly fry the paste, and then add the other filling ingredients in succession, stirring constantly. Set aside.

Place a nugget of the filling at the center of each wonton wrapper. Fold the square in half diagonally to make a triangle. Use a little water to seal the sides. Deep-fry the stuffed wonton until golden brown, drain on paper towels, and serve with the sweet chili sauce.

Preparation time: 10 minutes   Cooking time: 5 minutes

fried sweet potato mantod

Food stalls in Thailand sell bananas and taro cooked in this way. (Taro is a tuber that is sometimes mixed with flavoring and served as a dessert.)

1 egg
3 tablespoons coconut milk
2 tablespoons all-purpose flour
1 tablespoon sugar
1/2 teaspoon salt
1 tablespoon sesame seeds
10 ounces sweet potato, peeled and cut into large wedges
  (about 2–2 1/2 cups)
Oil, for deep-frying

In a large bowl, combine the egg, coconut milk, flour, sugar, salt, and sesame seeds and mix well. Add the sweet potato wedges and stir until they are well coated.

Heat the oil and deep-fry the battered wedges until golden brown. Drain well before serving.

Preparation time: 5 minutes   Cooking time: 5 minutes

deep-fried yellow bean paste baa yir

For the sweet sauce
1/4 cup sugar
6 tablespoons rice vinegar
1/2 teaspoon salt

For the paste
2/3 cup dried mung beans, soaked in water for 30 minutes
  and drained
1 tablespoon all-purpose flour
2 teaspoons red curry paste
1 tablespoon light soy sauce
1 teaspoon sugar
2 Kaffir lime leaves, rolled into a thin cylinder and finely sliced
  into slivers
Oil, for deep-frying

To make the sauce, gently heat the sugar, vinegar, and salt until the sugar dissolves. Let cool before serving.

In a mortar, pound the drained mung beans to form a paste. Add the other ingredients in succession, stirring well. Pluck a small piece of the paste and form into a ball the size of a walnut. Do not mold too tightly. Deep-fry the balls in hot oil until golden brown, drain, and serve with the thick sweet sauce.

Preparation time: 5 minutes   Cooking time: 5 minutes

steamed mussels with galangal
hoy ob ka

This is the Thai version of steamed mussels and we consider it tastier than European versions. I hope you do too!

1 pound mussels
2 ounces fresh galangal, peeled and julienned (about $^1/_4$–$^1/_3$ cup)
6 Kaffir lime leaves, roughly chopped

For the sauce
2 tablespoons sugar
4 small fresh red chilies, lightly crushed
3 tablespoons fish sauce
3 tablespoons lemon juice

Scrub the mussels thoroughly under cold running water, scraping off any barnacles or beards. Put the mussels in a heavy pot on high heat. Throw in the galangal and Kaffir lime leaves, stirring thoroughly, then cover the pan. Leave for a moment, then lift and shake the pan to toss the mussels and mix the ingredients. Repeat this process for 5–8 minutes or until the shells have opened. Discard any mussels that have not opened.

To make the sauce, mix all the ingredients in a bowl and set aside.

Ladle the cooked mussels onto a serving dish and serve with the sauce. You can eat the galangal, taking a little with each mussel.

Preparation time: 10 minutes   Cooking time: 8 minutes

oysters with spicy dressing
hoy nang lom manow

6 oysters
Crushed ice
Cilantro, for garnishing

For the dressing
3 tablespoons lime juice
1 teaspoon sugar
2 garlic cloves, finely chopped
2 fresh red or green chilies, finely chopped
Salt, to taste

Shuck the oysters, removing them from the shells and slipping them into a bowl. Rinse the shells thoroughly, dry them, and set aside.

To make the dressing, place all the ingredients in a bowl, mix thoroughly, and set aside.

Place the oysters back in their shells and arrange them on the crushed ice. Spoon the dressing over them, then garnish with cilantro and serve.

Preparation time: 10 minutes

deep-fried shrimp and corn cakes
tod man kung

20 whole black peppercorns

3 garlic cloves

1/2 teaspoon salt

1 large dried red chili, finely chopped

Fresh corn kernels from 3 uncooked corncobs

8 ounces (peeled weight) raw shrimp, chopped (about 1–1 1/2 cups)

1 tablespoon fish sauce

1 teaspoon sugar

Oil, for deep-frying

Plum sauce (see page 25), for serving

In a mortar, pound together the peppercorns, garlic, salt, and dried chilies to form a paste. Add the corn and pound well into the paste. Add the raw shrimp, fish sauce, and sugar and pound well.

You should now have a thick paste, which you mold into about ten round patties approximately 2 inches in diameter. In a pan or deep-fryer, heat the oil to 400°F and deep-fry the patties in batches until golden brown, then drain. Serve hot with plum sauce.

Preparation time: 8 minutes   Cooking time: 5 minutes

corn cakes
tod man khao pod

8 ounces corn kernels (about 1 cup), canned or frozen; if canned, drain well

1 tablespoon curry powder

2 tablespoons rice flour

3 tablespoons all-purpose flour

1/2 teaspoon salt

2 tablespoons light soy sauce

Oil, for deep-frying

For the sauce

1/4 cup rice vinegar

2 tablespoons sugar

1-inch piece of cucumber, quartered lengthwise, then finely sliced

2 shallots, finely sliced

1 tablespoon ground roasted peanuts

1 small fresh red or green chili, finely sliced

To make the sauce, heat the vinegar and sugar together in a small pan, stirring constantly, until the sugar dissolves and the mixture begins to thicken slightly. Remove from the heat and let cool. Pour into a bowl, add the remaining ingredients, and stir thoroughly. Set aside.

In another bowl, mix together the corn, curry powder, flours, salt, and soy sauce. Heat the oil until a light haze appears. Take a tablespoon of the mixture and shape into a small patty, then slide it into the hot oil. Fry until golden brown. Continue until you have used all the mixture. Remove the cakes from the oil and drain. Serve hot with the sauce.

Preparation time: 8 minutes   Cooking time: 5 minutes

crab and coconut cakes with plum sauce

tod man poo

8 ounces fresh crabmeat (about 1 cup)

1 ounce dry unsweetened coconut (about ½ cup)

1 egg

2 garlic cloves, finely chopped

1 tablespoon fish sauce

1 tablespoon oyster sauce

Pinch of ground white pepper

Fine dried white bread crumbs, for coating

Oil, for deep-frying

For the plum sauce

1 preserved plum

6 tablespoons rice vinegar

¼ cup sugar

2 small fresh red or green chilies, finely chopped

To make the sauce, use a fork to scrape the plum flesh from the pit. Heat the vinegar and add the sugar and plum flesh, stirring until the sugar dissolves. Simmer until a thin syrup begins to form, then remove from the heat. Stir in the chilies, pour into a bowl, and set aside.

In a mixing bowl, stir together the crabmeat, coconut, egg, garlic, sauces, and pepper. Knead with your fingers, then form into small patties. Roll in the bread crumbs until well coated.

Heat a pan of oil to 400°F. Deep-fry the patties until golden brown. Drain on paper towels and serve with the plum sauce.

Preparation time: 10 minutes   Cooking time: 5 minutes

deep-fried spareribs with chili and lemongrass
gra dook moo tod

If you have a barbecue, you can use it instead of a deep-fryer.

2 tablespoons sesame oil

2 garlic cloves, finely chopped and crushed

1 lemongrass stalk, finely chopped and pounded

4 small fresh red chilies, finely chopped and pounded

1/2 teaspoon salt

1 teaspoon sugar

2 tablespoons fish sauce

1 pound pork spareribs, chopped into 2-inch pieces
  (ask your butcher to prepare them)

Oil, for deep-frying

For the lime dip

1/2 teaspoon salt

1 teaspoon ground white pepper

1/4 cup lime juice

Mix the sesame oil, garlic, lemongrass, chilies, salt, sugar, and fish sauce. Add the sparerib pieces, mix, and marinate for at least one hour.

Heat the oil and deep-fry the spareribs in batches until golden brown. Remove from the oil, drain, and keep warm until they are all done.

While the spareribs are frying, make the lime dip. Mix all the ingredients together and pour into a dipping bowl. Place the spareribs on a plate and serve with the dip.

Preparation time: 10 minutes   Cooking time: 5 minutes

broiled spicy sliced steak
nua nam tok

The Thai name for this dish translates as "beef waterfall." This is because when you eat it in Thailand, you perspire so much you look like a waterfall! If you don't like it too hot, reduce the chili powder.

Lettuce, cucumber, radish, and cilantro, for garnishing

8 ounces lean beefsteak

1/4 cup beef broth

2 tablespoons fish sauce

3 tablespoons lemon juice

1 teaspoon chili powder

1 teaspoon sugar

2 shallots or 1 onion, finely sliced

1 tablespoon ground brown rice

Arrange the lettuce, cucumber, radish, and cilantro leaves on a serving plate.

Preheat the broiler and when it is hot, broil the steak quickly—the meat should be rare in the middle. Slice it thinly and set aside.

Put the broth, fish sauce, lemon juice, chili powder, and sugar in a small pan over a high heat. Stir quickly and bring to a boil. Add the steak slices and stir; add the shallots or onion and stir, then add the ground rice and stir once to mix. Cook for a few seconds, then scoop the mixture onto the prepared plate and serve.

Preparation time: 5 minutes   Cooking time: 8 minutes

steamed spareribs with black bean sauce

gra dook moo nueng dow jeow

2 pounds small pork spareribs, chopped into 1-inch pieces
  (ask your butcher to prepare them)

1 teaspoon salt

1 tablespoon sugar

2 teaspoons black bean sauce

2 garlic cloves, finely chopped

2 teaspoons cornstarch

2 long fresh chilies (1 red and 1 green), finely sliced

In a large bowl, mix the rib pieces with the rest of the ingredients, making sure each piece is coated with the mixture. Divide the mixture between four to six small serving bowls.

Using your largest steamer (or your largest pan with enough room for all the bowls of ribs), steam the ribs in their bowls for 20–25 minutes and serve.

Preparation time: 5 minutes   Cooking time: 25 minutes

spicy shrimp
pla gung

This can be made with any combination of seafood.

2 tablespoons vegetable broth
2 tablespoons fish sauce
1/2 teaspoon chili powder
6 large raw shrimp, peeled and deveined
1 lemongrass stalk, finely chopped
3 shallots, coarsely chopped
4 Kaffir lime leaves, finely sliced
1 teaspoon sugar
2 tablespoons lemon juice
2 scallions, finely chopped

Boil the broth, fish sauce, and chili powder in a small pan. Add the shrimp and cook quickly until they are opaque.

Add the remaining ingredients, stir well, remove from the heat, and transfer to a serving plate.

Preparation time: 5 minutes   Cooking time: 3 minutes

fried shrimp with
sesame seeds
kung chup bang tod

The batter and dipping sauce can also be used for vegetables such as carrots, celery, and zucchini.

Oil, for deep-frying
12 large raw shrimp, deheaded, peeled, tails left on, and deveined

For the batter
1 cup all-purpose flour
1/2 teaspoon salt
1 egg
1 tablespoon sesame seeds

For the dipping sauce
3 tablespoons light soy sauce
1/2 teaspoon sugar
5–6 cilantro leaves, coarsely chopped

In a bowl, mix the flour and salt. Break the egg into the mixture and mix thoroughly. Add 1 cup of water and the sesame seeds gradually, whisking constantly. You should have a thick, creamy batter.

Heat the oil until a light haze appears. Dip each shrimp into the batter, ensuring it is well coated, and drop into the hot oil. Deep-fry until golden brown. Remove from the oil, drain, and place on a serving dish.

To make the dipping sauce, mix the soy sauce with the sugar and chopped cilantro leaves in a small bowl. Serve with the shrimp.

Preparation time: 5 minutes   Cooking time: 3 minutes

barbecued shrimp on lemongrass
kung hoh takrai

1¼ pounds medium size raw shrimp, peeled and deveined

4 garlic cloves, crushed

4 scallions, chopped

2 teaspoons sugar

2 teaspoons fish sauce

2 teaspoons cornstarch

1 strip of bacon, finely chopped

10 fresh lemongrass stalks, each about 5½ inches long

Plum sauce (see page 25), for serving

Put the shrimp, garlic, scallions, sugar, fish sauce, cornstarch, and bacon in a food processor and blend until fine and pasty. With lightly oiled hands, mold level tablespoons of the shrimp mixture around the center of each lemongrass stalk.

Heat a greased barbecue, grill pan, or broiler until hot and cook the stalks until the shrimp mixture is cooked through, turning occasionally during cooking. Serve with the plum sauce.

Preparation time: 5 minutes   Cooking time: 8 minutes

shrimp wrapped in noodles
gung sarong

1 egg

½ teaspoon salt

½ teaspoon sugar

½ teaspoon ground white pepper

6 raw jumbo shrimp, peeled and deveined

1 nest of ba mee noodles (egg noodles)

Oil, for deep-frying

Sweet chili sauce (see page 17) or plum sauce (see page 25),
  for serving

In a bowl, mix the egg, salt, sugar, and white pepper together. Add the shrimp and mix well. Lift three or four strands of noodles and wrap them around each shrimp, winding the strands into a mesh that thickly covers the shrimp.

In a pan or deep-fryer, heat the oil until a light haze appears (about 400°F), and deep-fry the wrapped shrimp until golden brown. Drain and serve with the sweet chili sauce or plum sauce.

Preparation time: 10 minutes   Cooking time: 3 minutes

hot-and-sour crispy calamari and lime salad yam pla muk grob

1 small lime

Oil, for deep-frying

7 ounces cleaned baby calamari, sliced into rings

30 sweet basil leaves

2 lemongrass stalks, trimmed of all tough leaves and finely chopped into rings

10 Kaffir lime leaves, rolled into a thin tube and finely sliced across

3/4 cup roasted peanuts

5 small fresh red or green chilies, finely chopped

1/2 teaspoon salt

Cut the lime into quarters. Remove and discard the core and any seeds. Dice the segments, with the skin, to make tiny cubes. Set aside.

Heat a pan of oil for deep-frying to 400°F. Using a mesh strainer, deep-fry the calamari until golden and crispy. Drain on paper towels and place in a large mixing bowl. Deep-fry the basil until crispy, drain, and place in the bowl. Repeat the process with the lemongrass and then the Kaffir lime leaves.

Add all the remaining ingredients, including the reserved lime cubes, to the bowl. Mix well, then turn onto a plate and serve.

Preparation time: 8 minutes   Cooking time: 10 minutes

crispy rice with pork, shrimp, and coconut sauce khao tang naa tang

2 garlic cloves, roughly chopped

1 teaspoon chopped cilantro root

1 teaspoon whole black peppercorns

4 ounces ground pork (about 1/2 cup)

2 ounces ground raw shrimp (about 1/3 cup)

2 tablespoons oil

2 shallots, finely chopped

1 cup coconut milk

1 tablespoon fish sauce

1 tablespoon light soy sauce

1 tablespoon tamarind water

1 teaspoon sugar

2 tablespoons ground roasted peanuts

1 large fresh red chili, sliced lengthwise, and fresh cilantro leaves, for garnishing

Crispy rice (see page 107), for serving

In a mortar, pound the garlic, cilantro root, and peppercorns together to form a paste. In a bowl, mix the ground pork and shrimp together. In a large pan, heat the oil and stir in the garlic paste. Add the mixed pork and shrimp and stir well. Stirring constantly, add each of the remaining ingredients in succession (apart from the garnish).

Turn onto a plate, garnish with chili and cilantro leaves, and serve with the crispy rice.

Preparation time: 10 minutes   Cooking time: 10 minutes

steamed scallops with garlic

hoy nung kratiem jeow

6 scallops in the shell, cleaned

3 tablespoons oil

3 garlic cloves, finely chopped

2 small fresh red or green chilies, sliced into fine rings

For the sauce

3 tablespoons light soy sauce

1-inch piece of fresh ginger, finely chopped

1 teaspoon sugar

1 small red chili, finely chopped

For the garnish

2 tablespoons scallion, finely sliced

6 cilantro leaves

Set the scallops in their shells in a steamer over 1–2 inches hot water. In a small frying pan, heat the oil, add the garlic, and fry until golden brown. Pour a spoonful of garlic and oil over each scallop, add a little sliced chili, cover, and steam over medium heat for 10–15 minutes until the scallops are cooked.

While the scallops steam, mix together all the sauce ingredients in a small bowl.

When the scallops are cooked, remove from the steamer, place on a serving dish, and garnish with the scallion and cilantro leaves. Serve the sauce on the side.

Preparation time: 5 minutes   Cooking time: 15 minutes

skewered marinated pork   moo ping

This dish can be prepared with chicken if preferred. It makes about a dozen skewers.

2 garlic cloves, finely chopped
6 cilantro roots, finely chopped
1/4 cup fish sauce
1 tablespoon light soy sauce
1/2 cup thick coconut cream
1/2 cup oil
1 tablespoon sugar
1/2 teaspoon ground white pepper
1 pound lean pork, thinly sliced into 3 x 1 1/2-inch pieces
Lettuce, parsley, or cilantro leaves, for garnishing

For the sauce
1 tablespoon fish sauce
2 tablespoons lemon juice
1 tablespoon light soy sauce
1 teaspoon chili powder
1 tablespoon sugar
1 tablespoon cilantro leaves, coarsely chopped

Combine all the skewer ingredients, except the pork and the garnish, in a bowl until they are thoroughly blended. Add the pork and mix in, making sure that each piece is well coated. Let stand for at least 30 minutes, longer if possible.

While the meat is marinating, place all the sauce ingredients in a small bowl and mix well. Check the taste; if too hot, add more fish sauce, lemon juice, and sugar.

Preheat the broiler. Take twelve 8-inch wooden skewers and thread two pieces of meat on each, making sure that as much of the surface of the meat as possible will be exposed to the broiler. (Assemble more skewers if you have meat left over.)

Broil under a high heat for 2–3 minutes each side or until the meat is completely cooked through. Serve on a dish garnished with lettuce, parsley, or cilantro, with the sauce on the side.

Marinating time: 30 minutes   Cooking time: 5 minutes

pork with fruit and peanuts
ma ho

This dish is an interesting contrast in both color and texture between the fruit (if you prefer, you can substitute pineapple for the tangerines) and meat mixture, topped with chilies and cilantro.

2 tangerines, peeled and separated into segments
1 tablespoon oil
2 garlic cloves, finely chopped
2 shallots, finely chopped
1/3 cup ground pork
1 tablespoon fish sauce
1 teaspoon sugar
2 tablespoons coarsely pounded roasted peanuts
1/2 teaspoon ground black pepper

For the garnish
2 fresh red chilies, seeded and cut into slivers
Cilantro leaves

Lay the tangerine segments in a dish. In a frying pan, heat the oil and fry the garlic and shallots until light brown. Add the pork, fish sauce, and sugar and stir-fry until the pork is cooked through. Stir in the peanuts and ground pepper and mix thoroughly. Remove from the heat.

Place a heaping teaspoon of the meat mixture on each tangerine segment. Garnish with red chilies and cilantro leaves.

Preparation time: 5 minutes   Cooking time: 5 minutes

chicken wings with lemongrass
gai ta krai

This is good with sticky rice and is perfect when traveling because it can be eaten cold.

3 lemongrass stalks, finely chopped
2 small fresh red chilies, finely chopped
1 pound chicken wings
3 tablespoons oyster sauce
1 tablespoon fish sauce
1 teaspoon sugar
Oil, for deep-frying
Sweet chili sauce (see page 17), to serve

In a large bowl, mix all the ingredients together. Let marinate for 15 minutes. Heat the oil to 400°F in a pan or deep-fryer and fry the chicken wings until golden brown. Drain and serve with the sweet chili sauce.

Marinating time: 15 minutes   Cooking time: 5 minutes

heavenly beef
nua sawan

In Thailand, after marinating the meat, we leave it in the sun to dry for a day.

¼ cup fish sauce
1 tablespoon palm sugar (jaggery) or brown sugar
2 teaspoons roughly pounded coriander seeds
1 pound lean tender beefsteak, thinly sliced
Oil, for deep-frying

In a saucepan, heat the fish sauce, then add the sugar and stir well until it has dissolved. Stir in the coriander seeds, mix well, then remove from the heat and let cool.

Place the beef slices in a bowl, add the fish sauce mixture, and mix well. Let marinate for at least one hour. Remove the meat and let it drain overnight on a rack set over a large plate.

Heat the oil to 400°F in a pan or deep-fryer and fry the dried meat until it is dark brown. Drain on paper towels and serve.

Marinating time: 1 hour   Cooking time: 5 minutes

fried beef balls
tord man nua

¾ cup ground beef
3 garlic cloves, chopped
1 small onion, finely chopped
½ teaspoon ground black pepper
1 tablespoon fish sauce
1 tablespoon light soy sauce
½ teaspoon sugar
1 egg
2 tablespoons finely chopped cilantro leaves
All-purpose flour, for coating
Oil, for deep-frying
Sweet chili sauce (see page 17), for serving

In a bowl, mix together the ground beef, garlic, onion, pepper, fish sauce, soy sauce, sugar, egg, and cilantro leaves until well blended. Form into firm balls an inch in diameter and lightly dust the balls with flour.

Heat the oil in a wok until a haze appears and deep-fry the balls until golden brown. Drain on paper towels and serve with chili sauce.

Preparation time: 3 minutes   Cooking time: 5 minutes

chicken satay

satay

1 teaspoon coriander seeds

1 teaspoon cumin seeds

3 skinless boneless chicken breasts

2 tablespoons light soy sauce

1 teaspoon salt

¼ cup oil

1 tablespoon curry powder

1 tablespoon ground turmeric

½ cup coconut milk

3 tablespoons sugar

For the peanut sauce

2 tablespoons oil

3 garlic cloves, finely chopped

1 tablespoon dry curry paste (see page 73)

½ cup coconut milk

1 cup chicken broth

1 tablespoon sugar

1 teaspoon salt

1 tablespoon lemon juice

¼ cup crushed roasted peanuts

Roast the coriander and cumin seeds gently in a small frying pan without oil for about 5 minutes, stirring and shaking to ensure they do not burn. Remove from the heat and grind together to make a fine powder. (You could use store-bought ground seeds if more convenient.)

With a sharp knife, cut the chicken breasts into fine slices about 3 x 1½ x ½ inches. Put the slices in a bowl and add all the remaining ingredients, including the ground coriander and cumin seeds. Mix thoroughly and let it marinate overnight or for eight hours (you can prepare in the morning for an evening meal).

To make the peanut sauce, heat the oil in a frying pan until a light haze appears. Add the chopped garlic and fry until golden brown. Add the curry paste, mix well, and cook for a few more seconds. Add the coconut milk, mix in well, and cook for a few seconds. Add the broth, sugar, salt, and lemon juice and stir to blend. Cook for 1–2 minutes, stirring constantly. Add the crushed peanuts, stir well, then pour the sauce into a bowl.

When you are ready to cook the chicken, preheat the broiler (Thais would normally use a charcoal or barbecue grill). Using 8-inch wooden satay sticks, thread two pieces of the marinated chicken on each stick—not straight through the middle of each piece, but in and out, as if you were gathering or smocking a piece of material. Broil the satays for about 6–8 minutes, until the meat is cooked through, turning to ensure they are browned on both sides. Serve with the peanut sauce.

Marinating time: 8 hours   Cooking time: 8 minutes

salads & soups

theater

Likay is a type of folk theater enjoyed by many people and is especially popular in the provinces, where it is still an important feature of many festivals. It is a burlesque form of the more sedate Lakhon (see page 14) and contains elements of pantomime, comic folk opera, and social satire (pictured at right and on previous pages). This kind of entertainment is generally performed against a simple painted backdrop at temple fairs.

The stories are usually derived from much-loved court dramas but have been embellished with local references and anecdotes. The dialogue is spontaneous, spiced with outrageous puns and double entendres. Each performance is accompanied by traditional music and dance, which some troupes like to exaggerate in a rather camp fashion. The costumes and makeup are often dramatic—Thai people talk of "dressing up like Likay" if they want to describe exaggerated clothing and makeup.

Likay theater is often an inspired combination of sources and styles, mixing words and music, costume and makeup, to create something unique for each performance. The ingredients for the food in this section are similarly thrown together, though in a more considered fashion, to give you flavorful salads and subtly balanced soups.

bamboo shoot salad

yam normai

This dish originates from Isaan, in the northeast of Thailand, where it would be eaten with sticky rice.

4 ounces bamboo shoots (about $^2/_3$–$^3/_4$ cup)

2 shallots, peeled

1 garlic clove, peeled

$^1/_4$ cup vegetable broth

2 tablespoons lemon juice

2 tablespoons light soy sauce

1 teaspoon sugar

1 teaspoon chili powder

2 teaspoons dry-fried sesame seeds

10 fresh mint leaves

1 scallion, finely chopped

2 large Chinese cabbage (Napa cabbage) leaves

2 long beans (also known as yard-long beans), chopped into 4-inch lengths (7 to 8 green beans may be substituted)

With a knife, scrape the pieces of bamboo shoot to make long matchstick gratings, and set aside.

Grill the shallots and garlic until they are soft and give off a pleasant, slightly burned aroma without actually burning. Place in a mortar and pound them together, then set aside.

Put the broth into a saucepan and bring to a boil. Add the bamboo shoot gratings, the pounded shallot and garlic, lemon juice, soy sauce, sugar, and chili powder and stir well. Remove from the heat. Add the sesame seeds, mint leaves, and scallion, stirring briefly. Arrange the Chinese cabbage leaves and the long beans around the edge of a serving dish, pour the mixture into the center, and serve.

Preparation time: 3 minutes   Cooking time: 5 minutes

green papaya salad
som tam

Som Tam is now as well known as Tom Yam and Pad Thai. If prepared with soy sauce, this is suitable for vegetarians.

4 ounces green papaya, peeled, seeds removed (about $3/4$–1 cup shredded)

1 garlic clove

3 small fresh red or green chilies

1 tablespoon roasted peanuts

1 ounce long beans, chopped into 1-inch lengths (about $1/4$ cup)
(green beans may be substituted)

2 tablespoons lemon juice

3 tablespoons light soy sauce or fish sauce

1 teaspoon sugar

1 medium tomato, chopped into segments

2 large Chinese cabbage (Napa cabbage) leaves

Finely shred the papaya flesh with a cheese grater or chop it very finely into long, thin shreds. Set aside.

In a mortar, lightly pound the garlic, add the chilies, and lightly pound again. Add the peanuts and lightly pound while occasionally stirring with a spoon to prevent the resulting paste from thickening. Add the long beans and slightly bruise them. Add the shredded papaya and lightly pound and stir until all the ingredients are blended together. Add the lemon juice, soy or fish sauce, and sugar and stir into the mixture. Finally, add the tomato, stirring once.

Put the cabbage leaves on a plate and scoop the mixture onto them.

Preparation time: 10 minutes

mango salad with cashews
yam mamuang

The difficulty with this dish is to find unripe green mangoes; otherwise it is delightfully easy to make. Use green cooking apples if you can't get ahold of the mangoes.

1 small green mango, peeled and grated or finely chopped

3 small fresh red or green chilies, finely chopped

3 shallots, finely chopped

1 teaspoon sugar

1 garlic clove, finely chopped

2 tablespoons lemon juice

$1/2$ teaspoon salt

2 tablespoons whole roasted cashews

Briefly soak the grated or chopped mango in cold water to remove any syrup. Drain and put in a large bowl along with all the other ingredients. Stir well and serve.

Preparation time: 3 minutes

wood ear mushroom salad

yam het hoo noo

When I was young, my mother used to make jellyfish salad, which I loved. When I came to live in Europe, it was impossible to find jellyfish, so I substituted mushrooms, as the texture is similar.

1 garlic clove

3 small fresh red or green chilies

1 teaspoon sugar

2 tablespoons lemon juice

2 tablespoons light soy sauce

2 ounces presoaked dried wood ear mushrooms, cut into strips ($^3/_4$–1 cup)

2 ounces celery, julienned (about 1 stalk)

1 ounce carrot, julienned (about $^3/_4$ cup)

1 ounce cucumber, julienned (3–4 tablespoons)

2 scallions, julienned

1 tablespoon crushed roasted peanuts

1 teaspoon dry-fried sesame seeds

1 shallot, finely chopped into rings

4–5 lettuce leaves

Cilantro leaves, for garnishing

In a mortar, pound the garlic and chilies until well crushed. Combine with the sugar, lemon juice, and soy sauce to make a sauce.

Place the mushrooms, celery, carrot, cucumber, and scallions in a bowl. Add the sauce and stir well. Add the peanuts, sesame seeds, and shallot rings and stir. Arrange the lettuce leaves on a serving dish and place the mixture on top. Garnish with cilantro leaves.

Preparation time: 10 minutes

vegetable salad with peanut sauce

salad kaek

This dish originates from the Muslim area in the south of Thailand and is vegetarian.

Oil, for deep-frying
2 blocks of tofu, about 2 inches square
4 ounces bean sprouts (about 1½–2 cups)
4 ounces long beans, chopped into 1-inch lengths (about 1 cup)
1 medium tomato, thinly sliced
4 ounces cucumber, thinly sliced (about ¾ cup)
4 ounces green cabbage (about 1½–2 cups), thinly sliced, then broken up into strands
2 hard-boiled eggs

For the sauce
2 tablespoons oil
1 tablespoon red curry paste
2 cups coconut milk
½ teaspoon salt
1 tablespoon sugar
1 teaspoon tamarind water
¼ cup crushed roasted peanuts

To make the sauce, heat the oil in a wok or large frying pan and stir in the curry paste. Add the coconut milk and stir well. Add all the remaining ingredients together, stirring constantly. Cook briefly until the coconut milk comes to a boil. Remove at once from the heat.

To make the salad, heat the oil to 400°F in a pan or deep-fryer and fry the tofu until golden. Remove, drain, and set aside.

Arrange all the vegetables in a salad bowl. Shell and quarter the eggs, then place them in the bowl. Thinly slice the tofu and add to the bowl.

Serve the salad with the sauce, either separately or poured over the salad and tossed.

Preparation time: 10 minutes   Cooking time: 15 minutes

chicken salad with mint and nuts

yam gai

This recipe is one of my grandmother's, and I have changed it little over the years.

6 ounces skinless boneless chicken breast

3 ounces bean sprouts (about 1¼–1½ cups)

3 ounces cucumber, cut in half lengthwise, seeded, and then julienned (about ½–¾ cup)

3 ounces onion, finely chopped (about ⅔–¾ cup)

2 tablespoons fish sauce

2 tablespoons lime juice

3 small fresh red or green chilies, roughly chopped

1 tablespoon finely chopped mint leaves

2 tablespoons ground roasted peanuts

2 tablespoons dry fried sesame seeds

Bring a pan of water to a boil, add the chicken breasts, and simmer until cooked through. Drain and let cool.

Shred the meat into small pieces into a bowl, allowing any liquid it may retain to fall into the bowl. Add all the remaining ingredients to the chicken and stir well. Turn onto a serving plate and serve.

Preparation time: 5 minutes   Cooking time: 15 minutes

chili salmon salad
laab pla

8-ounce salmon fillet, shredded

2 tablespoons fish sauce

2 tablespoons lemon juice

1 teaspoon sugar

1 teaspoon chili powder

1 teaspoon finely chopped lemongrass

1 teaspoon finely chopped Kaffir lime leaves

1 scallion, finely chopped into rings

10 mint leaves

1 head of Belgian endive

Dip the salmon in boiling water to blanch it. Remove and drain. Place in a large mixing bowl and add all the remaining ingredients except for the Belgian endive. Stir well.

Arrange the Belgian endive leaves on a serving dish and spoon the chili salmon mixture onto the leaves just before serving.

Preparation time: 5 minutes   Cooking time: 2 minutes

cucumber and shrimp
salad
yam taeng gwa

8 raw jumbo shrimp, peeled, deveined, and cut in half lengthwise

6 ounces cucumber, peeled and finely sliced (about 1 cup)

4 shallots, finely chopped

2 small fresh red chilies, finely chopped

1 medium tomato, cut into segments

2 tablespoons fish sauce

2 tablespoons lemon juice

1 teaspoon sugar

1 tablespoon roasted sesame seeds

Cook the shrimp in boiling water for 3 minutes, then remove and let cool.

In a large salad bowl, mix all the remaining ingredients along with the cooked shrimp. Stir well, turn onto a serving plate, and serve.

Preparation time: 3 minutes   Cooking time: 3 minutes

tuna salad
yam platuna

6 large lettuce leaves

4 ounces canned tuna in oil (about 1 cup)

1 tablespoon finely chopped fresh ginger

1 young lemongrass stalk, thinly sliced

6 small red shallots, thinly sliced

2 small fresh red chilies, finely chopped

1 tablespoon fish sauce

1 tablespoon lime juice

1 teaspoon sugar

2 scallions, roughly chopped

Arrange the lettuce leaves on a serving platter and set aside. Flake the tuna into a bowl, add all the remaining ingredients, and mix well. Turn the mixture onto the lettuce-lined platter and serve.

Preparation time: 3 minutes

beef and eggplant salad
yam nua makua

I first had the idea for this recipe while I was watching a cooking program on Thai television.

7 round green Thai eggplants, cut in half, then finely sliced

1 teaspoon salt, dissolved in a bowl of water

8 ounces tender boneless beef, finely sliced

4 shallots, finely sliced

2 small fresh red chilies, roughly chopped

2 tablespoons fish sauce

1 teaspoon sugar

2 tablespoons lemon juice

20 mint leaves

As you slice the eggplants, place them in the bowl of salted water. This keeps the eggplants from turning brown. Drain the slices when you are ready to use them.

In a saucepan, heat ¼ cup of water, then add the beef and cook quickly until the meat is opaque and cooked through. Add the eggplants, shallots, chilies, fish sauce, and sugar, stirring briskly. Remove from the heat and add the lemon juice and mint leaves, continuing to stir quickly. Place the mixture on a serving dish and serve.

Preparation time: 5 minutes   Cooking time: 10 minutes

seafood salad
yam talay

2 garlic cloves, very finely chopped

4 small fresh red or green chilies, very finely chopped

2 tablespoons crushed roasted peanuts

1 tablespoon sugar

3 tablespoons fish sauce

3 tablespoons lime juice

Lettuce leaves

1 small onion, thinly sliced and separated into rings

2 ounces pineapple segments (about 1/3–1/2 cup)

2 ounces baby calamari, chopped into small rings (about 1/2 cup)

2 ounces raw shrimp, peeled, deveined, and cut in half lengthwise (about 1/2 cup)

2 ounces shelled mussels (about 1/2 cup)

2 ounces shelled baby clams (about 1/2 cup)

2 ounces fish balls, cut in half (about 1/2 cup)

Cilantro leaves, to garnish

In a bowl, mix the garlic, chilies, peanuts, sugar, fish sauce, and lime juice to make a dressing. Set aside. Place the lettuce leaves, onion rings, and pineapple segments in a large bowl and set aside.

In a saucepan, heat a cupful of water, add the calamari, shrimp, mussels, and baby clams and cook quickly. Drain, then place all the seafood, including the fish ball halves, into a pan, add the prepared dressing, and heat, stirring rapidly for the brief time it takes to cook the ingredients, probably no more than a minute. Scoop the mixture into the salad in the large bowl, toss well, garnish with cilantro, and serve.

Preparation time: 10 minutes   Cooking time: 5 minutes

hot-and-sour pickled
cabbage salad
yam pak dong

This can be served with rice soup or as a side dish with curries.

6 ounces pickled cabbage, finely chopped (about 3/4 cup)

2 garlic cloves, finely chopped

4 shallots, finely chopped

4 small fresh hot red or green chilies, finely chopped

1 teaspoon sugar

2 tablespoons roasted peanuts, crushed

In a bowl, mix all the ingredients together. Place the mixture in a serving dish and serve.

Preparation time: 3 minutes

crispy fish with mango
yam pla krop

In Thailand we use river catfish, which is thin and very easy to fry.

6 large lettuce leaves
Oil, for deep-frying, plus 1 tablespoon
3 small red shallots, finely sliced
1 medium trout or similar firm fish, cleaned and filleted

For the dressing
1 green mango, finely sliced into small wedges
1 carrot, julienned
1 celery stalk, julienned
1 tablespoon fish sauce
1 tablespoon lime juice
1 teaspoon sugar
3 small fresh red chilies, finely chopped

Arrange the lettuce leaves on a serving platter and set aside.

Heat the oil and fry the shallots until crispy. Set aside.

Heat the tablespoon of oil and fry the whole trout fillets until crispy. Drain on paper towels, then flake the fish into bite-size pieces. Place on the lettuce and set aside.

Mix all the dressing ingredients in a bowl, pour them over the fish, and garnish with the crispy shallots.

Preparation time: 5 minutes   Cooking time: 15 minutes

sweet-and-sour soup with tofu
gaeng preowan tao hou

2 cups vegetable broth

2 teaspoons all-purpose flour

2 tablespoons pickled cabbage, chopped into 1-inch lengths

1 ounce bamboo shoots, julienned (about 1/4 cup)

4-ounce cake soft white tofu, cut into 1/4-inch cubes

1 ounce sweet red peppers, seeded and finely chopped
   (about 2–3 tablespoons)

2 scallions, finely chopped

2 tablespoons light soy sauce

1 tablespoon vinegar

1 teaspoon sugar

1/2 teaspoon ground white pepper

In a large pan, bring the broth to a boil and stir in the flour to thicken slightly. Add the rest of the ingredients in succession, stirring constantly. Transfer to a serving bowl and serve.

Preparation time: 5 minutes   Cooking time: 5 minutes

cauliflower, coconut, and galangal soup
tom ka

1/2 cup coconut milk

1-inch piece of lemongrass, finely chopped into rings

1-inch piece of fresh galangal, finely chopped into rings

3 Kaffir lime leaves, roughly torn into quarters

1 small cauliflower, cut into florets

2 tablespoons light soy sauce

1 teaspoon sugar

3 cups vegetable broth

4 small fresh red or green chilies, slightly crushed

2 tablespoons lemon juice

Cilantro leaves, for garnishing

In a large pan, heat the coconut milk with the lemongrass, galangal, Kaffir lime leaves, cauliflower, soy sauce, sugar, and broth and simmer until the cauliflower florets are al dente.

Remove from the heat and add the chilies and lemon juice. Stir once, pour into a serving bowl, and garnish with cilantro leaves.

Preparation time: 5 minutes   Cooking time: 8 minutes

mixed vegetable soup
jap chai

1 garlic clove, roughly chopped

2 cilantro roots, roughly chopped

1/2 teaspoon whole black peppercorns

2 tablespoons oil

2 ounces green cabbage, finely shredded (about 1 cup)

2 ounces daikon (white radish), cut into 1-inch cubes
(about 1/4–1/2 cup)

2 broccoli florets with stems, coarsely chopped

1 celery stalk, coarsely chopped

5 cups vegetable broth

4-ounce cake fried tofu, cut into 1-inch cubes
(about 1–1 1/2 cups)

2 tablespoons light soy sauce

1 tablespoon dark soy sauce

1 teaspoon sugar

In a mortar, pound the garlic, cilantro roots, and peppercorns to
form a paste.

In a pan, heat the oil and briefly fry the paste. Add the vegetables
and stir-fry briefly. Pour the broth over the vegetables and bring to
a boil.

Add all the remaining ingredients and simmer gently until the
vegetables are well cooked.

Preparation time: 5 minutes   Cooking time: 10 minutes

vermicelli soup
gaeng wun sen

Bean curd skins look like wrinkled brown paper and can be bought in
packages from Asian markets. They are very fragile and should be
soaked for 5 minutes before you shred them.

1 garlic clove, finely chopped

1 tablespoon oil

3 cups vegetable broth

1/4 cup ground pork, roughly shaped into small balls

2 ounces presoaked dried wood ear mushrooms, coarsely chopped
(about 3/4–1 cup)

2 ounces bean curd skin fragments, soaked, then drained
(about 1 1/4 cups)

4 ounces vermicelli noodles, coarsely chopped (about 2–2 1/2 cups)

2 scallions, cut into 1-inch lengths

1 teaspoon tang chi (preserved radish)

1 tablespoon fish sauce

1 tablespoon light soy sauce

1/2 teaspoon sugar

1/2 teaspoon ground white pepper

Cilantro leaves, for garnishing

Make the garlic oil by frying the garlic in the oil until golden brown,
then set aside. Bring the broth to a boil, add all the remaining
ingredients except the cilantro leaves, and simmer briefly.

Ladle into serving bowls and pour a little garlic oil into each. Garnish
with the cilantro leaves and serve.

Preparation time: 5 minutes   Cooking time: 5 minutes

omelette soup
gaeng kaijeow

2 tablespoons oil

1 egg, beaten

3 cups vegetable broth

1 carrot, chopped into small cubes

1 teaspoon tang chi (preserved radish)

2 scallions, cut into 1-inch lengths

2 tablespoons light soy sauce

1/2 teaspoon sugar

1/2 teaspoon ground white pepper

Cilantro leaves, for garnishing

Heat the oil in a small omelette pan, add the egg, and cook to make a firm omelette. Remove the omelette from the pan, roll into a cylinder, and cut into ¼-inch-thick slices. Secure each round omelette slice with a tiny skewer or toothpick to hold it together, and set aside.

Put the broth and carrot into a large pan and bring to a boil. Simmer for 5 minutes, then add all the remaining ingredients except the cilantro leaves, ending with the omelette slices. Stir, then ladle into serving bowls and garnish with the cilantro leaves.

Preparation time: 10 minutes   Cooking time: 15 minutes

fish ball soup with basil leaves
gaeng krapow

3 cups chicken broth

1 tablespoon light soy sauce

1 tablespoon fish sauce

1 medium onion, cut in half, then finely sliced

6 ounces fish balls

1 small fresh red chili, finely chopped

15 holy basil leaves

In a saucepan, bring the broth gently to a boil. Add the soy sauce, fish sauce, onion, fish balls, and chili. Cook for 5 minutes, remove from the heat, and add the basil leaves.

Ladle the soup into bowls and serve.

Preparation time: 3 minutes   Cooking time: 5 minutes

wonton soup geo nam

3 garlic cloves, finely chopped

¹/₄ cup ground pork

Salt and ground black pepper

6 wonton wrappers

2 cups chicken broth

1 teaspoon tang chi (preserved radish)

1 tablespoon fish sauce

1 tablespoon light soy sauce

¹/₂ teaspoon sugar

1 scallion, sliced into fine rings

Mix together the garlic, pork, and a sprinkling of salt and pepper.
Put an equal portion of this mixture in the center of each wonton
wrapper. Gather up the corners and squeeze together to make a little
purse. Set aside.

In a saucepan, heat the broth and add the tang chi. Bring to a boil.
Add the wonton purses, along with all the remaining ingredients
except for the scallion. Return to a boil, stirring gently.

Remove from the heat and pour into a tureen. Sprinkle the scallion
rings on top, add salt and pepper to taste, then serve.

Preparation time: 5 minutes   Cooking time: 5 minutes

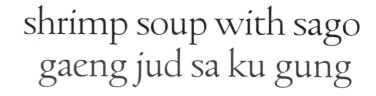

shrimp soup with sago
gaeng jud sa ku gung

Sago is a starch made from the pith of the sago palm. When boiled, the hard, semitransparent, whitish grains expand into little balls of sweet, transparent jelly.

2^1/$_2$ cups vegetable broth
2 tablespoons sago
2 ounces presoaked dried wood ear mushrooms, roughly sliced (about ^{3}/$_4$–1 cup)
1 small onion, sliced into thin strips
1 small carrot, julienned
1 teaspoon tang chi (preserved radish)
6 ounces raw shrimp, peeled and deveined (about 1–1^1/$_2$ cups)
2 tablespoons fish sauce
1 teaspoon sugar
^{1}/$_2$ teaspoon ground white pepper

For the garnish
1 scallion, finely chopped into rings
Cilantro leaves

In a large pan, bring the broth to a boil, add the sago, and simmer until the hard sago "nuts" have become soft and clear. Add all the remaining ingredients, stirring briefly.

Ladle into serving bowls and garnish with the scallion rings and cilantro.

Preparation time: 5 minutes   Cooking time: 8 minutes

spicy soup with shrimp and lemongrass
tom yam kung

This is probably the best-known dish in Thai cooking. Tom yam is a basic method of making soup and you can use it with other ingredients besides shrimp: mussels, scallops, crab claws, chicken pieces, or thinly sliced beef. The aroma of the soup is created by the main ingredients, a mixture of lemongrass, lime leaves, and fresh chili.

2 1/2 cups chicken broth
1 lemongrass stalk, chopped into 4 pieces and slightly crushed
4 Kaffir lime leaves, roughly chopped
2 small fresh red chilies, finely sliced
8 small button mushrooms, quartered
8 raw jumbo shrimp, peeled and deveined
2 tablespoons fish sauce
2 tablespoons lime juice
1 teaspoon sugar
Cilantro leaves, for garnishing

In a saucepan, heat the broth to boiling point. Add the lemongrass, Kaffir lime leaves, chilies, and mushrooms and return to a boil. Add the shrimp, fish sauce, lime juice, and sugar and simmer for about a minute or so, until the shrimp are cooked.

Ladle into soup bowls and garnish with the cilantro.

Preparation time: 5 minutes   Cooking time: 5 minutes

corn and shrimp soup
gaeng chud kaopot

2 1/4 cups chicken broth
1 cup canned creamed corn
6 ounces small shrimp (about 1 cup)
1 egg, beaten
1 tablespoon fish sauce
1 tablespoon soy sauce
1/2 teaspoon black pepper
1 tablespoon chopped cilantro leaves

In a large saucepan, bring the chicken broth and corn to a boil. Add the shrimp, pour in the beaten egg, and stir to break up the egg in the soup. Add the fish sauce, soy sauce, and black pepper. Bring back to a boil and cook for 1 minute.

Pour into a soup tureen, sprinkle with the chopped cilantro leaves, and serve.

Preparation time: 3 minutes   Cooking time: 5 minutes

hot-and-sour chicken and shallot soup
tom kong

2¹/4 cups chicken broth

4 whole chicken wings, bones left in, roughly chopped
   into 1-inch pieces

5 shallots, peeled

2 large dried red chilies

2 tablespoons fish sauce

1 tablespoon lemon juice

1 teaspoon sugar

20 sweet basil leaves

Preheat the broiler.

In a saucepan, heat the broth to boiling point. Add the chicken pieces and return to a boil, then let it simmer.

Meanwhile, place the shallots and the chilies under the broiler until the chilies start to blacken, and turn them once. Transfer the broiled shallots and chilies to a board. With the handle or side of a large kitchen knife, crush them until they split open. Add the crushed shallots and chilies to the pan of broth and continue to simmer until the chicken pieces are cooked through.

Add the fish sauce, lemon juice, sugar, and basil leaves. Stir quickly and serve at once.

Preparation time: 3 minutes   Cooking time: 15 minutes

ground pork and mushroom soup
gaeng chud moo sap

8 whole black peppercorns

2 garlic cloves

3 cilantro roots

1/2 cup ground pork

5 cups chicken broth

4 dried Chinese mushrooms, soaked in hot water, stems removed,
   finely sliced

1 tablespoon fish sauce

1 tablespoon light soy sauce

2 scallions, finely chopped

In a mortar, pound the peppercorns, garlic, and cilantro roots until they form a paste.

In a bowl, mix together the ground pork and the paste until well blended, then form into small balls.

In a saucepan, heat the chicken broth. Add the meatballs, mushrooms, fish sauce, and light soy sauce. Bring to a boil, then remove from the heat and add the scallions just before serving.

Preparation time: 3 minutes   Cooking time: 5 minutes

pork, potato, and shallot soup
tom jiew

2¹/4 cups chicken broth

6 ounces tender boneless pork, cut into 1-inch cubes (about ³/4 cup)

4 ounces potato, cut into 1-inch cubes (about ³/4–1 cup)

2 shallots, finely sliced lengthwise

1 tablespoon tamarind water

2 tablespoons fish sauce

1 teaspoon sugar

2 small fresh red or green chilies, slightly crushed with the side of a kitchen knife

20 sweet basil leaves

In a large pan, heat the chicken broth to boiling point. Add all the remaining ingredients and simmer until the potato is al dente. Pour into a soup tureen and serve.

Preparation time: 8 minutes   Cooking time: 10 minutes

beef with bean sprouts
koawleaw nua

1 clove garlic, finely chopped

1 tablespoon oil

4 cups beef broth

2 garlic cloves, roughly crushed

3 cilantro roots

1 star anise

8 ounces beef tenderloin, cut into ¹/4-inch-thick pieces (about 1 cup)

3 tablespoons light soy sauce

2 tablespoons fish sauce

2 teaspoons sugar

¹/2 teaspoon ground white pepper

1¹/2 cups bean sprouts

1 scallion, finely chopped, for garnishing

First make some garlic oil: fry the garlic in the oil until golden brown, then set aside.

In a saucepan, heat the broth to boiling point. Add the garlic, cilantro roots, and star anise and return to a boil. Add the beef, light soy sauce, fish sauce, sugar, and pepper and return to a boil. Place the bean sprouts in the boiling stock for just five seconds, stirring well.

Ladle the hot soup into serving bowls. Sprinkle with the chopped scallion and a teaspoon of garlic oil.

Preparation time: 5 minutes   Cooking time: 10 minutes

sparerib and tamarind soup
tom som

1 teaspoon whole black peppercorns
1 teaspoon finely chopped cilantro root
1 garlic clove, peeled
2 small shallots, peeled
1 tablespoon oil
2¹/₄ cups chicken broth
1 pound small pork spareribs, chopped into 1-inch pieces
1-inch piece of fresh ginger, julienned
2 tablespoons tamarind water
1 tablespoon sugar
2 tablespoons fish sauce
2 scallions, cut into 1-inch lengths

In a mortar, pound together the peppercorns, cilantro root, garlic, and shallots until they form a paste.

In a large saucepan, heat the oil and fry the paste for just 5 seconds, stirring constantly. Add the broth and bring it to a boil, stirring well. Add the spareribs and return to a boil. Add all the remaining ingredients. Return to a boil again and simmer for 1 minute. Ladle into bowls and serve.

Preparation time: 5 minutes   Cooking time: 8 minutes

curries & main dishes

music

Traditional Thai music has unique qualities that cannot be found anywhere else. Its exotic and wondrous sounds are very appealing to foreign visitors. Among the many styles of Thai music that still manage to maintain a traditional air about them are *Luk Thung* and *Mor Lum*. These are the Thai equivalents of country music, and with their distinctive Thai flavor, they are hugely popular in rural areas. The photographs on the opposite page and on previous pages show performances of folk music.

Luk Krung is the musical style of the city, and many new, young groups and bands have made this a rapidly growing industry. In fact, Thais have all styles of popular music: jazz, rock, rap, and hip-hop.

When I was young I always wanted to be on the stage, but my mother wouldn't allow it, telling me that I would have no future and no prospects. Nowadays in Thailand, parents encourage their children to be entertainers from a young age. Teenage boys in country villages dream about becoming either pop singers or Thai boxers (*Muay Thai*), in much the same way as boys in the West want to be rock stars or baseball players.

In this chapter, I want to demonstrate the inventiveness of Thai cuisine and how we have kept the traditions of Thai food alive with modern adaptations. Much as with music, you will find that our food encompasses a wide range of flavors and styles, and is constantly updated and diversified.

Curry pastes

These are the recipes for the curry pastes most commonly used in Thai cooking. You can, of course, buy most of these pastes in any Asian market.

red curry paste
gaeng pet

8 long dried red chilies, seeded and chopped

1 teaspoon ground coriander seeds

¹/₂ teaspoon ground cumin seeds

1 teaspoon ground white pepper

2 tablespoons chopped garlic

2 lemongrass stalks

3 cilantro roots, chopped

1 teaspoon chopped Kaffir lime zest or finely chopped lime leaves

1-inch piece of fresh galangal, chopped

2 teaspoons shrimp paste

1 teaspoon salt

Using a mortar and pestle or a spice grinder, blend all the ingredients into a paste. There should be about ¼ cup.

Preparation time: 8 minutes

dry curry paste
gaeng panaeng

10 long dried red chilies, seeded and chopped

5 shallots, chopped

2 tablespoons chopped garlic

2 lemongrass stalks, chopped

1-inch piece of fresh galangal, chopped

1 teaspoon ground coriander seeds

1 teaspoon ground cumin seeds

3 cilantro roots, chopped

1 teaspoon shrimp paste

2 tablespoons roasted peanuts

Using a mortar and pestle or a spice grinder, blend all the ingredients into a paste. There should be about ⅛ cup.

Preparation time: 8 minutes

green curry paste
gaeng keow wan

2 long fresh green chilies, seeded and chopped

10 small fresh green chilies, seeded and chopped

1 tablespoon chopped lemongrass

3 shallots, chopped

2 tablespoons chopped garlic

1-inch piece of fresh galangal, chopped

3 cilantro roots, chopped

1 teaspoon ground coriander seeds

½ teaspoon ground cumin seeds

½ teaspoon ground white pepper

1 teaspoon chopped Kaffir lime zest or finely chopped lime leaves

2 teaspoons shrimp paste

1 teaspoon salt

Using a mortar and pestle or a spice grinder, blend all the ingredients into a paste. There should be about 3 tablespoons.

Preparation time: 8 minutes

vegetable curry
gaeng pa

2 tablespoons oil

1 tablespoon red curry paste (see page 72)

1 ounce krachai (fingerroot), peeled and julienned
  (about 2 tablespoons)

2¼ cups vegetable broth

2 ounces long beans, cut into 1-inch pieces (about ⅓–½ cup)

2 ounces carrots, julienned (about ⅓–½ cup)

2 ounces baby corn (about 4–6 cobs), cut into 1-inch pieces

3 Kaffir lime leaves, roughly chopped

2 large fresh red or green chilies, roughly chopped

2 tablespoons light soy sauce

1 teaspoon sugar

½ teaspoon salt

4 round green Thai eggplants, quartered

20 basil leaves

In a saucepan, heat the oil and quickly stir in the curry paste. Add
the krachai and the vegetable broth and stir briefly, then add all the
remaining ingredients except the basil. Stir well. Add the basil leaves,
stir once, and then ladle into bowls and serve.

Preparation time: 5 minutes   Cooking time: 5 minutes

potato curry
gaeng kari

1 teaspoon coriander seeds

2 teaspoons finely chopped galangal

2 teaspoons finely chopped lemongrass

2 teaspoons finely chopped garlic

2 tablespoons oil

1 cup coconut milk

8 ounces potatoes, cut into 1-inch cubes (about 1½–1¾ cups)

2 tablespoons light soy sauce

1 teaspoon sugar

½ teaspoon salt

1 tablespoon curry powder

½ cup vegetable broth

8 ounces small onions (about 2 cups), cut in half

In a mortar, pound together the coriander seeds, galangal,
lemongrass, and garlic to form a paste.

In a saucepan, heat the oil, stir in the paste, and immediately add
the coconut milk. Stir briefly, then add the potatoes, soy sauce,
sugar, salt, and curry powder; stir well. Bring to a boil and add the
vegetable broth. Return to a boil, add the onion halves, and simmer
until the potatoes are al dente.

Preparation time: 5 minutes   Cooking time: 10 minutes

spicy quick-fried long beans
pat prik king

Oil, for deep-frying, plus 2 tablespoons
3 ounces tofu, finely sliced (about ¾–1 cup)
1 teaspoon finely chopped garlic
1 tablespoon red curry paste (see page 72)
8 ounces long beans, cut into 1-inch pieces (about 1½–2 cups)
2 tablespoons light soy sauce
¼ cup vegetable broth
1 teaspoon sugar
1 tablespoon ground roasted peanuts
2 Kaffir lime leaves, finely chopped

In a pan or deep-fryer, heat the oil to 400°F and fry the tofu in the hot oil until the white sides are golden brown. Drain and set aside.

In a wok or frying pan, heat the 2 tablespoons of oil, fry the garlic until golden brown, then stir in the red curry paste. Add all the remaining ingredients, finishing with the tofu. Stir briefly and serve.

Preparation time: 5 minutes   Cooking time: 15 minutes

sweet-and-sour vegetables
pat preow wan

1 teaspoon cornstarch
2 tablespoons oil
1 teaspoon finely chopped garlic
2 cobs of baby corn
8–10 pineapple chunks
1 small chunk cucumber, quartered, then cut into thick slices
1 onion, cut in half, then sliced into thin segments
1 tomato, quartered
2 medium scallions, cut into 1-inch lengths
2 large fresh red chilies, sliced diagonally
2 tablespoons light soy sauce
1 teaspoon sugar
½ teaspoon ground white pepper

Mix the cornstarch with ¼ cup water and set aside.

In a wok or frying pan, heat the oil and fry the garlic until golden brown. Add each of the remaining ingredients one at a time, stirring constantly. Add the cornstarch and water mixture, stirring briefly to thicken, then turn onto a serving dish.

Preparation time: 5 minutes   Cooking time: 5 minutes

fried bamboo shoots with egg
pat normai

2 tablespoons oil

1 teaspoon finely chopped garlic

4 ounces skinless boneless chicken breast, finely sliced (about $^1/_2$ cup)

1 egg

*8 ounces bamboo shoots, diagonally sliced $^1/_4$ inch thick
(about $1^1/_4$–$1^3/_4$ cups)*

1 onion, cut in half, then chopped into thin slices

2 medium scallions, finely cut into rings

2 ounces oyster mushrooms, thinly sliced (about $^1/_2$ cup)

1 tablespoon light soy sauce

1 tablespoon fish sauce

$^1/_2$ teaspoon sugar

$^1/_2$ teaspoon ground white pepper

Cilantro leaves, for garnishing

In a wok or frying pan, heat the oil and fry the garlic until golden brown. Add the chicken, stir, and cook until the meat is slightly opaque. Break the egg into the pan, spreading the broken yolk a little. Before the egg sets, throw in the bamboo shoots, onion, scallions, and mushrooms and stir rapidly. Add the remaining ingredients, except the cilantro, continuing to stir rapidly, and then turn onto a serving dish. Garnish with the cilantro and serve.

Preparation time: 3 minutes   Cooking time: 15 minutes

mushrooms with ginger
pat king

2 tablespoons oil

1 teaspoon finely chopped garlic

*2 ounces presoaked dried wood ear mushrooms, coarsely
chopped if large (about $^3/_4$–1 cup)*

1 onion, cut in half, then chopped into thin slices

1 carrot, julienned

$^1/_2$ sweet red pepper, julienned

2-inch piece of fresh ginger, julienned

2 medium scallions, finely chopped

1 tablespoon light soy sauce

1 teaspoon yellow bean sauce

$^1/_2$ teaspoon sugar

$^1/_4$ cup vegetable broth

Cilantro leaves, for garnishing

In a wok or frying pan, heat the oil and fry the garlic until golden brown. Add all the remaining ingredients, except the cilantro leaves, one at a time, stirring constantly. Turn onto a serving dish and garnish with the cilantro.

Preparation time: 5 minutes   Cooking time: 3 minutes

morning glory curry
gaeng te po

Morning glory (water spinach) has a taste that is similar to spinach, and it is a common ingredient in Thai cooking. It is easily recognizable by its arrow-shaped leaves.

2 tablespoons oil
1 garlic clove, finely chopped
1 tablespoon red curry paste (see page 72)
1 cup coconut milk
4 ounces oyster mushrooms, chopped (about 1 cup)
4 ounces fried tofu, sliced into 2 x 1/2-inch strips (about 1 cup)
3 Kaffir lime leaves, coarsely chopped
1 small Kaffir lime, cut in half
1/2 teaspoon salt
1 tablespoon tamarind water (or 2 tablespoons lemon juice)
1 tablespoon light soy sauce
1 teaspoon sugar
1/2 cup vegetable broth
2 ounces (about 1 cup) morning glory (water spinach),
  chopped into 1-inch lengths

In a frying pan or wok, heat the oil and fry the garlic until golden brown. Stir in the curry paste and immediately add the coconut milk, stirring well. Add the remaining ingredients one at a time, except the broth and morning glory, stirring constantly. Bring to a boil, add the vegetable broth, and return to a boil. Add the morning glory and simmer until cooked.

Preparation time: 10 minutes   Cooking time: 8 minutes

pork curry with morning glory
pra ram rong song

6 ounces (about 2 1/2–3 cups) morning glory (water spinach),
  chopped into 2-inch lengths
8 ounces boneless lean pork, finely slivered (about 1 cup)
2 tablespoons oil
2 garlic cloves, finely chopped
1 tablespoon dry curry paste (see page 73)
1 tablespoon fish sauce
1 tablespoon light soy sauce
1 teaspoon sugar
5 tablespoons coconut milk
2 tablespoons ground roasted peanuts

Bring a pot of water to a boil, blanch the morning glory for 2 minutes, then drain, reserving the cooking water. Arrange on a serving dish. Cook the pork in the reserved water for about 5 minutes, drain, and arrange on the morning glory; set aside.

In a frying pan, heat the oil and fry the garlic until golden brown. Add the curry paste, fish sauce, light soy sauce, and sugar and mix thoroughly. Add the coconut milk and ground roasted peanuts, stirring well. Bring to a boil, pour it over the pork and morning glory, and serve.

Preparation time: 5 minutes   Cooking time: 15 minutes

fried fish with chilies and tamarind sauce
pla lat prik

2 large garlic cloves, finely chopped

2 large fresh red chilies, finely chopped

1 medium firm-fleshed fish suitable for deep-frying
  (e.g., red snapper or sea bass)

Oil, for deep-frying, plus 2 tablespoons

2 tablespoons palm sugar (jaggery) or white sugar

3 tablespoons fish sauce

2 tablespoons tamarind water (or 1/4 cup lemon juice)

In a mortar, pound the garlic and chilies together. Set aside.

Rinse the fish and pat dry. In a pan or deep-fryer, heat the oil for deep-frying, then fry the fish until golden and crispy. Drain and place on a serving dish. Keep hot.

Heat 2 tablespoons oil in a wok or frying pan, then stir in the garlic and chili mixture. Add the sugar and stir, then stir in the fish sauce and tamarind water. Pour it over the fish and serve.

Preparation time: 5 minutes   Cooking time: 10 minutes

crab with chili
bu pad prik

4 fresh medium crabs

1 tablespoon finely chopped ginger

3 garlic cloves, finely chopped

4 fresh red or green chilies, finely chopped

1/4 cup oil

2 tomatoes, sliced

1 tablespoon fish sauce

1 tablespoon light soy sauce

1 teaspoon sugar

To prepare the crabs, remove the undershell and discard the abdominal sac just behind the mouth. Break off the pincers and crack them open. With a large knife, quarter each crab. Set aside.

In a mortar, pound together the ginger, garlic, and chilies to make a paste. Heat the oil in a wok or frying pan and stir in the paste. Stir in the tomatoes and 2 tablespoons water. Add the crab pieces, fish sauce, soy sauce, and sugar and stir well, ensuring that the crab is cooked and the pieces are well coated. Turn onto a serving platter and serve.

Preparation time: 10 minutes   Cooking time: 10 minutes

baby clams with dry curry
hoy pat pet

2 tablespoons oil

2 garlic cloves, finely chopped

2 teaspoons red curry paste (see page 72)

1 pound baby clams in the shell

2 tablespoons fish sauce

1 tablespoon light soy sauce

1 teaspoon sugar

3 round green Thai eggplants, quartered
  (if unavailable, use a third of a regular eggplant)

2 small Kaffir lime leaves, finely sliced

10 holy basil leaves

In a wok or frying pan, heat the oil, add the garlic, and fry until golden brown. Add the curry paste, mix, and cook for a few seconds.

Add the baby clams and cook briefly. Stirring constantly, add the remaining ingredients, pausing after the addition of the eggplants to give them a few seconds to cook.

When the clams are cooked through and opaque, give a final stir, pour the mixture into a warm serving dish, and serve.

Preparation time: 5 minutes   Cooking time: 5 minutes

scallops with vegetables
and oyster sauce
hoy pad nam mun hoy

2 tablespoons oil

2 garlic cloves, finely chopped

8 scallops, shelled

4–6 cobs of baby corn, quartered

2 ounces broccoli, chopped into small florets (about 1 heaping cup)

2 ounces celery, finely sliced (about $1/2$–$3/4$ cup)

2 ounces carrots, julienned (about $1/3$–$1/2$ cup)

2 tablespoons oyster sauce

$1/2$ teaspoon sugar

Ground white pepper, to taste

In a frying pan, heat the oil and fry the garlic until golden brown. Add the scallops and stir-fry briefly, then add all the other ingredients one at a time, except the pepper, stirring well between each addition. Sprinkle with the pepper and serve.

Preparation time: 5 minutes   Cooking time: 5 minutes

shrimp with holy basil
kung pad krapow

This recipe can be adapted by substituting pork or chicken for the shrimp, but the meat should be very finely chopped or coarsely ground.

2 tablespoons oil
2 garlic cloves, finely chopped
2 small fresh red or green chilies, finely chopped
6–8 raw jumbo shrimp, peeled and deveined
1 medium onion, cut in half and roughly sliced
2 tablespoons fish sauce
1 tablespoon light soy sauce
1 teaspoon sugar
20 holy basil leaves

In a wok or frying pan, heat the oil and fry the garlic and chilies, stirring well, until the garlic begins to brown. Add the shrimp and stir, then add the remaining ingredients, mixing well. Cook until the shrimp are opaque and cooked through. Turn onto a serving dish and serve.

Preparation time: 5 minutes   Cooking time: 10 minutes

fried shrimp with red
curry paste
chu chee kung

2 large dried red chilies, finely chopped
8 small red shallots, finely chopped
1 tablespoon red curry paste (see page 72)
2 tablespoons oil
2 tablespoons roasted peanuts, crushed
8 ounces raw shrimp, peeled and deveined
8 ounces long beans, cut into 1-inch lengths (about 1^{1}/2–2 cups)
^{1}/2 cup coconut milk
^{1}/2 teaspoon salt
1 teaspoon sugar

In a mortar, pound together the chilies and shallots. Add the curry paste and mix well.

Heat the oil in a wok or frying pan and briefly fry the paste. Add the peanuts and shrimp. Stir well, until the shrimp are opaque and cooked through, then add the long beans, coconut milk, salt, and sugar. Stir well for a few seconds, then place into a serving bowl and serve.

Preparation time: 5 minutes   Cooking time: 5 minutes

steamed fish with lemongrass
pla neung ta-krai

1 sea bass (about 1 pound), scored diagonally on both sides
4 lemongrass stalks, roughly crushed
Cilantro leaves, for garnishing

For the sauce
4 garlic cloves, finely chopped
3 small fresh red or green chilies, finely chopped
3 tablespoons fish sauce
1/4 cup lime juice
2 teaspoons sugar

Place the fish on a bed of lemongrass on a steaming tray and steam over boiling water for about 15 minutes until cooked.

To make the sauce, combine the garlic, chilies, fish sauce, lime juice, and sugar in a bowl.

To serve, arrange the fish on a serving dish, pour the sauce over it, garnish with cilantro, and serve.

Preparation time: 5 minutes   Cooking time: 15 minutes

fried chili shrimp with tamarind sauce
kung makham

2 tablespoons oil
1 large garlic clove, finely chopped
2 teaspoons grated fresh ginger
1 large fresh red chili, cut into small strips
2 tablespoons tamarind water (or 1/4 cup lemon juice)
1 tablespoon sugar
20 raw tiger shrimp, peeled and deveined
2 tablespoons fish sauce
Cilantro leaves, for garnishing

In a wok or frying pan, heat the oil and fry the garlic until golden. Add the ginger, chili, tamarind water, and sugar, stirring well. Add the shrimp and fish sauce, stirring well until the shrimp are opaque and cooked through.

Turn onto a serving dish, garnish with the cilantro, and serve.

Preparation time: 5 minutes   Cooking time: 5 minutes

chicken curry with bamboo shoots
gaeng normai gai

2 tablespoons vegetable oil

1 large garlic clove, finely chopped

1 tablespoon red curry paste (see page 72)

1 cup coconut milk

2 tablespoons fish sauce

1 teaspoon sugar

6 ounces skinless boneless chicken breast, finely sliced
(about 3/4 cup)

1/2 cup chicken broth

4 ounces bamboo shoots, cut into thin slices

3 Kaffir lime leaves, finely sliced

3 large fresh red chilies, sliced lengthwise

20 holy basil leaves

In a wok or frying pan, heat the oil and fry the garlic until golden brown. Add the curry paste and cook briefly, stirring well. Stir in half the coconut milk, the fish sauce, and the sugar. Add the chicken and stir well, then add the chicken stock and bamboo shoots. Stir again. Add the remaining coconut milk, the lime leaves, and the chilies. Stir and cook until the chicken is cooked through.

Add the basil leaves, stir, and cook gently for 1 minute, then turn onto a serving dish and serve.

Preparation time: 5 minutes   Cooking time: 5 minutes

chicken fried with cashews and dried chilies
gai pad med mamuang hin ma pan

2 tablespoons oil

2 garlic cloves, finely chopped

8 ounces skinless boneless chicken breast, finely sliced (about 1 cup)

1 tablespoon fish sauce

4 long dried chilies, sliced into rings

2 heaping tablespoons roasted cashews

1 tablespoon oyster sauce

1/2 teaspoon sugar

In a frying pan, heat the oil and fry the garlic until golden brown. Add the chicken, stir, and cook until the meat is slightly opaque.

Stirring after each addition, add the remaining ingredients, cook until the chicken is cooked through, and serve.

Preparation time: 3 minutes   Cooking time: 6 minutes

southern chicken curry

gaeng kolae

A *kolae* is a type of boat used by fishermen in the south of Thailand, which is where this dish originates.

1/4 cup oil

2 large garlic cloves, finely chopped

1 chicken (3–4 pounds), roughly chopped into 10–12 large pieces

2 cups coconut cream

2 1/4 cups chicken broth

1/4 cup fish sauce

2 tablespoons sugar

1/4 cup lime juice

10 small fresh red or green chilies, thinly sliced, for garnishing

For the curry paste

5 large dried red chilies, seeded and soaked in water for 5 minutes

1/2 teaspoon salt

1 teaspoon roughly chopped lemongrass

1/2 teaspoon coriander seeds

1/2 teaspoon cumin seeds

1 teaspoon dried shrimp paste

To make the curry paste, place all the ingredients in a mortar and pound together.

In a wok or frying pan, heat the oil and fry the garlic until golden brown. Add the chicken and fry until golden. Remove from the oil and set aside.

Pour the oil from the wok into a large saucepan, heat, and add the prepared paste, stirring until it begins to blend. Add half the coconut cream and stir well, then add the browned chicken and mix thoroughly. Add the remaining coconut cream and stir. Add the chicken broth and fish sauce and stir, then add the sugar and lime juice and stir well, bringing the liquid to a boil. Reduce the heat and simmer for 15 minutes.

Turn into a serving bowl and serve garnished with the chilies.

Preparation time: 10 minutes   Cooking time: 20 minutes

chicken pineapple curry
gaeng kua sapparot

1 tablespoon oil

2 garlic cloves, finely chopped

1 tablespoon red curry paste (see page 72)

6 ounces skinless boneless chicken breast, finely sliced
(about $^3/_4$ cup)

1$^1/_4$ cups coconut milk

1 small fresh pineapple, peeled, cored, and cut into small segments

3 Kaffir lime leaves, finely chopped

2 tablespoons lemon juice

2 teaspoons sugar

1 teaspoon salt

In a wok or frying pan, heat the oil and fry the garlic until golden brown. Add the curry paste and chicken and fry briefly, stirring, then add the coconut milk, stirring well. Slowly bring to a boil, then add the remaining ingredients, stirring constantly until the chicken is cooked through. Turn into a serving bowl and serve.

Preparation time: 5 minutes   Cooking time: 10 minutes

chicken curry with
pickled garlic
gaeng haeng lay

1 tablespoon oil

1 tablespoon red curry paste (see page 72)

6 ounces skinless boneless chicken breast, roughly sliced
(about $^3/_4$ cup)

$^1/_2$ teaspoon ground turmeric

$^1/_4$ cup coconut cream

2 tablespoons water

3 ounces (about 1$^1/_4$–1$^1/_2$ cups) presoaked dried Chinese mushrooms,
coarsely chopped

1 tablespoon lemon juice

1 tablespoon fish sauce

1 teaspoon sugar

$^1/_2$ teaspoon salt

1-inch piece of fresh ginger, julienned

1 whole head of pickled garlic, finely sliced across the bulb to make
flower-shaped sections

In a wok or frying pan, heat the oil and briefly stir in the curry paste. Add all the other ingredients one at a time, stirring briefly between each addition. Once the chicken is cooked through, immediately turn into a bowl and serve.

Preparation time: 5 minutes   Cooking time: 10 minutes

beef with asparagus and oyster sauce

nua pad nam man hoy

2 tablespoons oil

2 garlic cloves, finely chopped

6 ounces beef, thinly sliced (about ³/4 cup)

6 ounces young thin asparagus (or any other crunchy vegetable such as broccoli), chopped into 2-inch lengths (about 1¹/2–2 cups)

2 tablespoons oyster sauce

1 tablespoon fish sauce

¹/2 teaspoon sugar

¹/2 teaspoon ground white pepper

In a wok or frying pan, heat the oil and fry the garlic until golden brown. Stirring constantly, add each of the remaining ingredients one at a time, stirring well between each addition. When the beef is cooked, turn onto a serving dish and serve.

Preparation time: 5 minutes   Cooking time: 5 minutes

green beef curry
gaeng keow wan nua

This is my mother's recipe. Whenever I eat it, I think of her.

2 tablespoons oil

2 garlic cloves, finely chopped

1 tablespoon green curry paste (see page 73)

8 ounces tender boneless beefsteak, finely sliced, retaining the fat
(about 1 cup)

1 cup coconut cream

1 cup beef broth

2 large fresh red chilies, sliced diagonally into thin ovals

2 tablespoons fish sauce

6 round green Thai eggplants, quartered

1 teaspoon sugar

20 sweet basil leaves

In a large saucepan, heat the oil and fry the garlic until golden brown. Stir in the curry paste, mixing well. Add the beef and stir-fry until just cooked through. Add the coconut cream and stir well, bringing to a boil. Add the stock and return to a boil, stirring constantly. Simmer for 5 minutes, stirring in all the remaining ingredients except the basil. Stir in the basil leaves just before pouring the curry into a serving bowl.

Preparation time: 5 minutes   Cooking time: 10 minutes

beef panaeng curry
gaeng panaeng

As the name suggests, this dish is of Malaysian origin, and is drier than most Thai curries.

1/2 cup coconut cream, plus 1 tablespoon for garnishing

2 tablespoons oil

1 garlic clove, finely chopped

1 tablespoon dry curry paste (see page 73)

6 ounces lean beef, diced (about 3/4 cup)

2 tablespoons fish sauce

1 teaspoon sugar

2 Kaffir lime leaves, very finely chopped

15 holy basil leaves

1 long fresh red chili, sliced lengthwise

In a small pan, gently heat the ½ cup of coconut cream, but do not let it boil; set it aside.

In a wok or frying pan, heat the oil until a light haze appears, add the garlic, and fry until golden brown.

Add the curry paste and stir-fry for a few seconds. Add the beef and stir-fry until it is lightly cooked. Add the hot coconut cream, stir well, then add the fish sauce and sugar, continuing to stir. Just before serving, stir in the lime leaves, holy basil, and chili. Turn into a serving bowl and garnish with a tablespoon of coconut cream.

Preparation time: 5 minutes   Cooking time: 5 minutes

stuffed omelette
kai yat sai

1 tablespoon oil
2 garlic cloves, finely chopped
4 ounces ground pork (about ¹/2 cup)
2 ounces onions, finely chopped (about ¹/2 cup)
2 ounces carrots, finely chopped (about ¹/3–¹/2 cup)
¹/2 cup green peas
1 tomato, finely chopped
2 tablespoons fish sauce
¹/2 teaspoon sugar
Pinch of ground black pepper

For the omelette
2 eggs
1 tablespoon oil

Heat the oil and fry the garlic until golden brown. Add the ground pork, stirring well. Add all the remaining ingredients one at a time, stirring constantly. Remove from the heat and set aside.

To make the omelette, beat the eggs. In a wok, heat the oil, turning the wok so that the oil coats the entire inner surface. Pour in the eggs and turn the wok to spread evenly. When the egg has cooked, pour the pork filling into the center. Fold in the sides of the omelette to make a square package. Cook for a moment longer, then slide carefully onto a serving dish to serve.

Preparation time: 10 minutes   Cooking time: 8 minutes

pork with garlic and peppercorns
moo tod kratiam prik thai sod

This dish is somewhat different from the norm in Thai cuisine, as it derives its heat from peppercorns rather than from chilies.

2 tablespoons oil
2 large garlic cloves, finely chopped
4 ounces lean pork, finely chopped (about ¹/2 cup)
1 tablespoon fish sauce
1 tablespoon light soy sauce
1 tablespoon dark soy sauce
¹/2 cup meat broth or water
Pinch of ground white pepper
10 fresh peppercorns

In a wok or frying pan, heat the oil until a light haze appears. Add the garlic and fry until golden brown. Add the pork and cook briefly, stirring constantly. Add the remaining ingredients one by one, stirring briefly between each addition. By now the pork should be cooked through. Turn the heat up for a few seconds to reduce the liquid to about 3 tablespoons.

Scoop into a serving dish and serve.

Preparation time: 3 minutes   Cooking time: 5 minutes

spicy tofu with ground pork
chu chee tao hou

This can be made into a vegetarian dish by omitting the meat, substituting light soy sauce for fish sauce, and using vegetable broth instead of chicken broth.

Oil, for deep-frying, plus 2 tablespoons
8 ounces tofu, cut into $^1/_2$-inch cubes (about 2 cups)
1 tablespoon red curry paste (see page 72)
4 ounces ground pork (about $^1/_2$ cup)
2 tablespoons fish sauce
1 teaspoon sugar
$^1/_4$ cup chicken broth
2 fresh Kaffir lime leaves, rolled up into a thin tube and sliced into fine slivers

In a pan or deep-fryer, heat the oil. Fry the tofu cubes until golden brown. Drain on paper towels and arrange on a serving dish. Set aside.

Heat the 2 tablespoons of oil in a wok or frying pan and briefly fry the curry paste, stirring constantly. Add the ground pork and stir-fry until it is no longer pink. Add the fish sauce, sugar, and broth, mixing well.

Add the Kaffir lime leaf slivers. Pour the sauce over the deep-fried tofu and serve.

Preparation time: 3 minutes   Cooking time: 3 minutes

fried pork with eggplant
moo pad makua

This is my favorite dish and I often order it in restaurants. I am usually able to judge the chef by how this dish is cooked.

2 tablespoons oil
2 garlic cloves, finely chopped
4 small fresh red or green chilies, finely chopped
6 ounces ground pork (about $^3/_4$ cup)
8 ounces long Thai eggplants, roughly sliced (or one small regular eggplant, thinly sliced)
2 tablespoons fish sauce
1 teaspoon sugar
20 sweet basil leaves

Heat the oil in a wok or frying pan and fry the garlic until golden brown. Add the chilies and stir well. Add the pork, stir, and then add the eggplants. Stir again, add the fish sauce and sugar, then stir-fry until the eggplant is just cooked through.

Add the basil leaves, stir thoroughly, then turn onto a serving dish and serve.

Preparation time: 5 minutes   Cooking time: 5 minutes

ground pork with curry paste and bamboo shoots
moo kua kling normai

2 tablespoons oil

2 garlic cloves, finely chopped

1 tablespoon red curry paste (see page 72)

$^1/_2$ teaspoon ground turmeric

6 ounces ground pork (about $^3/_4$ cup)

4 ounces bamboo shoots, finely sliced (about 1 cup)

1 tablespoon fish sauce

1 tablespoon light soy sauce

1 teaspoon sugar

5 fresh Kaffir lime leaves, rolled up into a thin tube and
 finely sliced

In a frying pan, heat the oil and fry the garlic until golden brown.
Add the curry paste, turmeric, and ground pork and stir-fry until
the meat is cooked through.

Add the bamboo shoots, fish sauce, light soy sauce, and sugar and
mix thoroughly. At the last moment, stir in the Kaffir lime leaves,
turn onto a serving dish, and serve.

Preparation time: 3 minutes   Cooking time: 3 minutes

noodles & rice

thai films

Thai cinemas now show the best of Thai, Chinese, and Western films. This cultural mix reminds me of my close friend, the film producer Tom Waller, who is half Thai and half English.

He recently worked on the production of Oliver Stone's *Alexander*, a multimillion-dollar epic about Alexander the Great that was partly filmed in Lopburi, Thailand.

With more than 500 local crew and hundreds of Thai soldiers playing Macedonian warriors, blockbuster films like this help to support the Thai film industry. But for about the same cost as *Alexander*'s catering budget for the extras alone, Tom Waller produced an independent movie in Thailand called *Butterfly Man*, an adventure about a young Englishman who falls in love with Thai massage, Thai cooking, and a beautiful Thai woman, played by Napakpapha Mamee Nakprasitte, who won a Best Actress award at Utah's Slamdunk independent film festival in 2003. Accolades like these have helped put Thai talent on the moviemaking map.

Most indigenous Thai films are rarely successful abroad; however, several new directors are making their mark at film festivals around the world. Influential directors such as Nonzee Nimibutr and Penek Ratanaruang have pioneered a new wave of modern Thai cinema and are often critically acclaimed overseas before they are at home.

The catering on Thai film sets often consists of a quick lunch served in take-out boxes. They are usually single-dish meals based on rice and noodles, but I want to show you that there is far more than just pineapple fried rice and pad Thai—here are exciting combinations and a wide range of flavors using the many types of noodles, steamed and sticky rice, vegetables, seafood, and meat.

rice
khao

Rice is the all-important food in Thailand. In the Thai language, the verb "to eat" is *kin khao*, which actually means "eat rice." Rice is completely central to Thai food. A Thai will always start by having a plate of rice; the other dishes are to accompany the rice, not vice versa as in the West. Thais will also feel uncomfortable if they don't eat rice once a day, no matter what else they may have eaten.

Traditionally, we Thais finish all the rice on our plates out of respect for the Mother Goddess of Rice and to acknowledge the hardship that farmers endure in cultivating their crops. After finishing the meal, appreciative diners will put their hands together to thank the rice for filling their stomachs.

The recipes in this chapter deal with variations on the fried-rice dishes that are popular throughout Thailand. Fried rice serves as a gentle introduction to Thai cuisine for the gastronomically timid and for those unaccustomed to highly spiced foods. *Kao Pad* (fried rice) is eaten for a quick meal at any time of the day.

boiled rice
khao suay

An experienced Thai cook varies the water quantity according to the age, and thus the dryness, of the rice; the amount below is a reasonable average.

2¹/2 cups Thai fragrant rice
2¹/2 cups water

Rinse the rice thoroughly in at least three changes of cold water, until the water runs clear. Drain the rice and put it in a heavy saucepan along with the measured water. Cover and quickly bring to a boil. Uncover and cook, stirring vigorously, until the water level is below that of the rice, whose surface will begin to look dry. Reduce the heat to as low as possible, cover the pan again, and steam for 20 minutes.

Alternatively, use a rice cooker—they are cheap, efficient, and make perfect rice with a minimum of fuss.

crispy rice
khao tang

If, when you are cooking the rice, a mishap occurs and you are left with rice stuck to the bottom of the pan, don't worry: nothing is wasted in Thai cooking. Let the pan cool down, then lift out the sheet of rice and dry it. Break it into three or four pieces. Heat a pan of oil for deep-frying and fry the rice pieces until they are golden brown and crisp. Drain on paper towels.

sticky or glutinous rice
khao niew

This is a broad short-grain rice, mostly white, although it can be brown or even black. It is the staple of northern Thailand, where, during the meal, it is plucked with the fingers, rolled into a ball, and used for scooping up the other food. It is also used throughout Thailand to make desserts. Sticky rice cannot be cooked in a rice cooker and needs to be soaked before cooking. Instructions for steaming the rice follow.

steamed sticky rice
khao niew neung

2¹/₂ cups sticky rice

Put the rice in a pan, cover with water, and soak for at least 3 hours or overnight if possible. Drain and rinse thoroughly. Line the perforated part of a steamer with a double thickness of cheesecloth and scoop the rice into it. Heat the water in the bottom of the steamer to boiling and steam the rice over medium heat for 30 minutes.

vegetarian fried rice
khao pad mang sa virad

2 tablespoons oil

2 garlic cloves, finely chopped

1/3–1/2 cup mixed cooked beans, e.g., snow peas and green beans

2 tablespoons diced carrot

2 tablespoons diced tomato

2 tablespoons diced pineapple

2 tablespoons light soy sauce

1 teaspoon sugar

1/2 teaspoon ground white pepper

1 3/4–2 cups boiled fragrant rice (see page 106)

Cilantro leaves, for garnishing

In a wok or frying pan, heat the oil and fry the garlic until golden brown. Stirring constantly, add each of the remaining ingredients one at a time, except for the cilantro leaves. Stir thoroughly until the rice is heated through, then turn onto a serving dish and garnish with the cilantro leaves.

Preparation time: 3 minutes   Cooking time: 5 minutes

pineapple fried rice
khao pad sapparot

2 tablespoons oil

2 tablespoons dried shrimp

2 garlic cloves, finely chopped

3 1/2 cups boiled fragrant rice (see page 106)

1 tablespoon fish sauce

1 tablespoon light soy sauce

1 teaspoon sugar

1 small pineapple, chopped into 1/2-inch cubes (reserve the shell)

3 shallots, coarsely chopped

1 large fresh red chili, finely sliced

1 scallion, coarsely chopped

1 sprig of cilantro, coarsely chopped, plus leaves, for garnishing

In a wok or frying pan, heat a tablespoon of the oil, add the dried shrimp, and fry until crispy. With a slotted spoon, remove the shrimp, drain, and set aside.

Add the remaining oil to the wok, heat, add the garlic, and fry until golden brown. Add the cooked rice and stir thoroughly.

Add the fish sauce, soy sauce, and sugar. Stir and mix thoroughly. Make sure the rice is heated through, then add the pineapple, shallots, chili, scallion, cilantro, and the crispy shrimp. Mix thoroughly and heat through.

Fill the pineapple shell with the mixture, garnish with the cilantro leaves, and serve.

Preparation time: 5 minutes   Cooking time: 5 minutes

fried rice with mushrooms and pickled cabbage
khao pad pak gat dong

2 tablespoons oil

2 garlic cloves, finely chopped

3 1/2 cups boiled fragrant rice (see page 106)

4 ounces firm mushrooms (such as oyster mushrooms),
  coarsely chopped (about 1–1 1/4 cups)

6 ounces pickled cabbage (about 3/4 cup)

1 tablespoon light soy sauce

1 teaspoon sugar

Black pepper, to taste

Heat the oil in a wok or large frying pan and fry the garlic until golden brown. Add all the remaining ingredients and stir-fry for about 30 seconds before turning out onto a serving dish.

Preparation time: 3 minutes   Cooking time: 3 minutes

fried rice with turmeric
khao pad kamin

2 tablespoons oil

1 garlic clove, finely chopped

1 small onion, diced

1 carrot, diced

1 teaspoon ground turmeric

1 3/4–2 cups boiled fragrant rice (see page 106)

1/2 teaspoon sugar

1 tablespoon light soy sauce

1/2 teaspoon chili powder

2 ounces fried tofu, quartered (about 1/2–3/4 cup)

For the garnish

1 scallion, cut into rings

1 medium tomato, cut into wedges

3-inch piece of cucumber, cut into 1/2-inch slices

In a wok or frying pan, heat the oil until a light haze appears. Add the garlic and fry until golden brown. Stirring constantly, add the onion, carrot, turmeric, and rice. Stir thoroughly. Add the sugar, light soy sauce, and chili powder. Stir thoroughly.

Add the tofu, stir, and turn onto a serving dish. Sprinkle with the scallion rings and arrange the tomato and cucumber at the side of the dish.

Preparation time: 3 minutes   Cooking time: 5 minutes

chicken with mushrooms and bamboo shoots on rice

khao na gai

3¹/2 cups boiled fragrant rice (see page 106)

2 tablespoons oil

2 garlic cloves, finely chopped

4 ounces skinless boneless chicken breast, finely sliced (about ¹/2 cup)

2 ounces bamboo shoots, sliced (about ¹/2 cup)

2 ounces straw mushrooms, cut in half (about ¹/2–³/4 cup)

1 tablespoon light soy sauce

2 tablespoons fish sauce

1 teaspoon sugar

1 tablespoon dark soy sauce

¹/4 cup chicken broth or water

1 tablespoon all-purpose flour, mixed with 2 tablespoons water

2 scallions, roughly chopped

Pinch of ground white pepper

Put the cooked rice on a serving dish and keep it warm. Heat the oil in a wok or frying pan and fry the garlic until golden brown. Add the chicken and stir-fry for a few seconds. Add the bamboo shoots and straw mushrooms and stir. Stirring quickly after each addition, add the light soy sauce, fish sauce, sugar, dark soy sauce, and broth. Add more broth if the mixture becomes dry.

Add a tablespoon of the flour and water mixture to the wok and stir until thoroughly blended to make a slightly thickened sauce, adding a little more broth or flour/water mixture if necessary. Add the chopped scallions and the pepper, stir quickly, and serve immediately over the cooked rice.

Preparation time: 5 minutes   Cooking time: 5 minutes

spicy fried rice with chicken
khao pad prik gai

2 tablespoons oil

2 garlic cloves, finely chopped

4 small fresh red chilies, finely sliced

4 ounces skinless boneless chicken breast, finely sliced (about $^1/_2$ cup)

1 tablespoon fish sauce

$^1/_2$ teaspoon sugar

1 tablespoon light soy sauce

$3^1/_2$ cups boiled fragrant rice (see page 106)

1 small onion, sliced

2 scallions, sliced into 1-inch lengths

Cilantro leaves, for garnishing

In a wok or frying pan, heat the oil and fry the garlic until golden brown. Add the chilies and chicken and stir quickly. Add the fish sauce, sugar, and light soy sauce, stir, and cook for a few seconds until the chicken is cooked through. Add the cooked rice and stir thoroughly. Add the onion and scallions and stir quickly to mix.

Turn onto a serving dish and garnish with the cilantro.

Preparation time: 3 minutes   Cooking time: 5 minutes

fried rice with shrimp and green curry paste
khao pad kiow wan gung

2 tablespoons oil

2 garlic cloves, finely chopped

1 tablespoon green curry paste (see page 73)

4 ounces raw shrimp, peeled and deveined (about 1 cup)

2 tablespoons fish sauce

$^1/_4$ teaspoon sugar

1 tablespoon light soy sauce

$3^1/_2$ cups boiled fragrant rice (see page 106)

1 sweet red pepper, seeded and sliced

2 scallions, sliced into 1-inch lengths

Cilantro leaves, for garnishing

In a wok or frying pan, heat the oil until a light haze appears. Add the garlic and fry until golden brown. Add the green curry paste and the shrimp and stir quickly. Add the fish sauce, sugar, and soy sauce, stir, and cook for a few seconds until the shrimp are opaque and cooked through. Add the cooked rice and stir thoroughly. Add the sweet pepper and scallions and stir quickly to mix.

Turn onto a serving dish and garnish with the cilantro.

Preparation time: 5 minutes   Cooking time: 5 minutes

fried rice with chicken and curry powder
khao pad karee gai

2 tablespoons oil

2 garlic cloves, finely chopped

1 teaspoon medium-hot curry powder

3 ounces skinless boneless chicken breast, finely sliced
(about 1/3–1/2 cup)

3 1/2 cups boiled fragrant rice (see page 106)

1 tablespoon light soy sauce

2 tablespoons fish sauce

1/2 teaspoon sugar

2 scallions, sliced into 1-inch lengths

1/2 small onion, finely sliced

Pinch of ground white pepper

In a wok or frying pan, heat the oil and fry the garlic until golden brown. Add the curry powder, stir, and cook for a few seconds. Add the chicken and cook for a minute or two until the meat is opaque. Add the cooked rice and stir thoroughly. Add the light soy sauce, fish sauce, and sugar, stirring after each addition. Cook together for a few seconds until you are sure the meat is cooked through and the rice is thoroughly reheated.

Turn onto a serving dish, garnish with the scallions and onion, and lightly sprinkle with pepper.

Preparation time: 3 minutes   Cooking time: 5 minutes

fried rice with pork and chilies
khao pad moo

2 tablespoons oil

2 garlic cloves, finely chopped

4 ounces lean pork, finely diced (about 1/2 cup)

1 egg

1 tablespoon fish sauce

1 teaspoon sugar

1 tablespoon light soy sauce

3 1/2 cups boiled fragrant rice (see page 106)

1 small onion, sliced

1/2 red or green bell pepper, seeded and sliced

1/2 teaspoon ground white pepper

1 scallion, green part only, sliced into 1-inch lengths

Cilantro leaves, for garnishing

In a wok or frying pan, heat the oil until a light haze appears. Add the garlic and fry until golden brown. Add the pork and stir quickly; break the egg into the pan and stir quickly. Add the fish sauce, sugar, and light soy sauce, then stir and cook for a few seconds until the pork is cooked through. Add the cooked rice and stir thoroughly. Add the onion, bell pepper, white pepper, and scallion and stir quickly to mix.

Turn onto a serving dish and garnish with the cilantro.

Preparation time: 3 minutes   Cooking time: 5 minutes

beef fried rice with basil leaves
khao pad krapow nua

2 tablespoons oil
2 garlic cloves, finely chopped
3 small fresh red chilies, finely chopped
4 ounces ground beef (about 1/2 cup)
2 tablespoons fish sauce
1/2 teaspoon sugar
1 tablespoon light soy sauce
1 3/4–2 cups boiled fragrant rice (see page 106)
1 small onion, sliced
20 holy basil leaves

In a wok or frying pan, heat the oil and fry the garlic until golden brown. Add the chilies and ground beef and stir quickly to mix. Add the fish sauce, sugar, and light soy sauce. Stir-fry until the beef is cooked through.

Add the cooked rice and stir thoroughly. Add the onion and basil leaves, stirring quickly. Turn onto a serving dish and serve.

Preparation time: 3 minutes   Cooking time: 5 minutes

sticky rice and pork and chili sauce
khao niew nam prik ong

2 tablespoons oil
2 garlic cloves, finely chopped
2 teaspoons red curry paste (see page 72)
3 ounces ground pork (about 1/3–1/2 cup)
1 large tomato, finely chopped
2 tablespoons fish sauce
1 tablespoon lemon juice
1 teaspoon sugar
Sticky rice (see page 107), for serving

In a wok or frying pan, heat the oil until a light haze appears. Add the garlic and fry until golden brown. Mix in the curry paste and cook together briefly. Add the pork and stir-fry until the meat loses its pink color.

Add the tomato, stir, and cook for a few seconds. Add the fish sauce, lemon juice, and sugar. Stir together for 2 minutes to thoroughly blend the flavors.

Scoop the mixture into a small bowl and serve with sticky rice.

Preparation time: 3 minutes   Cooking time: 8 minutes

noodles
gueyteow

Noodles are a Chinese invention, but have become the basic fast food of most of Asia. In Thailand there are noodle sellers everywhere, more or less at any time of the day or night.

Noodles are made from either rice flour or soybean flour, and there are six main varieties.

Sen Yai
Sometimes called "rice river noodles" or "rice sticks," these are broad, flat noodles made of white rice flour. If bought fresh, the strands need to be separated before cooking.

Sen Mee
A small, wiry noodle, sometimes called "rice vermicelli."

Sen Lek
A medium-sized, flat rice flour noodle. The city of Chantaburi is famous for these noodles, which are sometimes called "Jantaboon noodles," after the nickname for the town.

Ba Mee
An egg and rice flour noodle, yellow in color, these come in a variety of shapes, each with its own name. However, it is unlikely that you will see anything other than the commonest form, which is like a thin spaghetti, curled up in nests, which need to be shaken loose before cooking.

Wun Sen
A very thin, wiry, translucent soybean flour noodle, also called "vermicelli" or "cellophane noodles."

Kanom Jin

The one uniquely Thai noodle, made from rice flour mixed with water, then squeezed through a special sieve to make thick strands like spaghetti. It is made only in large quantities for special occasions, usually temple festivals. Luckily, there is a very similar Japanese noodle, *longxu*, which is sold dried in packages and can be found in Asian markets.

Dried Noodles

All dried noodles, with the exception of ba mee noodles, need to be soaked in cold water for about 20 minutes before cooking (wun sen noodles need a little less time). The dry weight will generally double with soaking. After soaking, drain the noodles before cooking. Cooking is generally a matter of dunking them in boiling water for two or three seconds.

the four flavors
kruang prung

While each noodle dish has its own distinctive taste, the final flavor is left to the diner, who can adjust it by sprinkling very small amounts of the four flavors on top. These are always put out in small bowls wherever noodles are served.

Chilies in Fish Sauce *(Prik Nam Pla)*

Four small fresh red or green chilies, finely chopped, in ¼ cup of fish sauce.

Chilies in Rice Vinegar *(Prik Nam Som)*

Four small fresh red or green chilies, finely chopped, in ¼ cup of rice vinegar.

The other two flavors served with noodles are sugar *(nam tan)* **and chili powder** *(prik pon)***.**

thai fried noodles
gueytoew pad thai

3 tablespoons oil

1 garlic clove, finely chopped

2 ounces fried tofu, cut into $^1\!/_2$-inch cubes (about $^1\!/_2$–$^3\!/_4$ cup)

1 egg

4 ounces dried sen lek noodles (rice sticks), soaked in water for
  20 minutes and drained

1 tablespoon finely chopped chi po (preserved turnip)

2 scallions, cut into 1-inch pieces

2 tablespoons chopped roasted peanuts

$1^1\!/_2$ cups bean sprouts

$^1\!/_2$ teaspoon chili powder

1 teaspoon sugar

2 tablespoons light soy sauce

1 tablespoon lemon juice

1 sprig of cilantro, coarsely chopped

1 lemon wedge

In a wok or frying pan, heat the oil and fry the garlic until golden
brown. Add the tofu and stir. Break the egg into the wok, cook for a
moment, then stir. Add the noodles, stir well, then add the chi po,
scallions, half the peanuts, and half the bean sprouts.

Stir well, then add the chili powder, sugar, light soy sauce, and lemon
juice. Stir well and scoop onto a plate. Sprinkle with the remaining
peanuts and the chopped cilantro sprig. Arrange the remaining bean
sprouts and lemon wedge on the side of the plate; these can be added
by the diner as desired.

Preparation time: 10 minutes   Cooking time: 5 minutes

fried noodles with
mushrooms
mee pad het jay

2 tablespoons oil

2 ounces onions, coarsely chopped (about $^1\!/_2$ cup)

4 ounces (wet weight) sen mee noodles (rice vermicelli),
  soaked in water for 20 minutes and drained

2 ounces wood ear mushrooms, soaked in water and drained,
  then coarsely chopped (about $^3\!/_4$–1 cup)

2 ounces celery, coarsely chopped (about $^1\!/_2$ cup)

2 ounces tomatoes, coarsely chopped (about $^1\!/_3$–$^1\!/_2$ cup)

2 tablespoons light soy sauce

1 tablespoon sugar

$^1\!/_2$ teaspoon ground white pepper

Cilantro leaves, for garnishing

Heat the oil in a wok or large frying pan and fry the onions briefly.
Add all the remaining ingredients except the cilantro, one at a time,
stirring between each addition.

As soon as the ground pepper is stirred in, turn the mixture onto a
serving plate, garnish with the cilantro, and serve.

Preparation time: 5 minutes   Cooking time: 3 minutes

egg noodles with stir-fried vegetables
mee sua

2 tablespoons oil

1 garlic clove, finely chopped

1 large dried red chili, roughly chopped

6 raw jumbo shrimp, peeled and deveined

4 ounces cooked egg noodles (about ²/₃–1 cup)

1 celery stalk, finely chopped

1 cup bean sprouts

2 scallions, finely chopped

1 medium tomato, cut into segments

1/2 teaspoon chili powder

2 tablespoons light soy sauce

1 tablespoon fish sauce

1/2 teaspoon sugar

In a wok or frying pan, heat the oil until a light haze appears. Fry the garlic, and after a moment, add the chili and continue stir-frying until the garlic is golden. Add the shrimp and cook briefly until they start to become opaque.

Add the noodles, stir well, then add all the remaining ingredients, stirring quickly. Turn onto a serving dish and serve.

Preparation time: 10 minutes   Cooking time: 3 minutes

deep-fried noodles with mixed vegetables
mee krop lad nah

1 nest of egg noodles

Oil, for deep-frying

For the mixed vegetables

2 tablespoons oil

1 garlic clove, finely chopped

2 ounces bamboo shoots, finely sliced (about 1/2 cup)

2 ounces straw mushrooms (about 1/3–1/2 cup)

4 cobs of baby corn, cut in half lengthwise

1 small red or green bell pepper, seeded and diced

2 scallions, chopped into 1-inch lengths

2 tablespoons light soy sauce

1 teaspoon dark soy sauce

1 teaspoon sugar

1/2 teaspoon ground white pepper

1 tablespoon cornstarch, mixed with 1/2 cup vegetable broth or water to make a thin paste

Cilantro leaves, for garnishing

Separate the strands of the egg noodles. In a pan or deep-fryer, heat the oil to 400°F and deep-fry the noodles until crisp. Remove from the oil and drain. Place the noodles on a serving dish and set aside.

Heat the oil in a wok or frying pan until a light haze appears. Fry the garlic until golden brown. Add the remaining ingredients, except for the cornstarch paste and cilantro, stirring constantly. Stir in the paste. Pour over the noodles, garnish with cilantro, and serve.

Preparation time: 5 minutes   Cooking time: 8 minutes

fried noodles with crab
mee pad pod

2 tablespoons oil

1 garlic clove, finely chopped

1 teaspoon red curry paste (see page 72)

4 ounces crabmeat (about 1/2 cup)

1 egg, lightly beaten

8 ounces(dry weight) sen mee noodles (rice vermicelli),
   soaked in water for 20 minutes and drained

1 cup bean sprouts

3 scallions, thinly sliced

1 tablespoon fish sauce

1 tablespoon light soy sauce

1 teaspoon sugar

1 large fresh red chili, finely chopped

2 tablespoons lime juice

Heat the oil in a wok or frying pan and fry the garlic until golden brown. Add the remaining ingredients one at a time, stirring well between each addition. Cook for another minute or two, turn onto a serving plate, and serve.

Preparation time: 3 minutes   Cooking time: 5 minutes

egg noodles with calamari
ba mee plamuk

1 nest of dried ba mee noodles (egg noodles)

6 ounces calamari, cleaned and roughly chopped (about $3/4$–1 cup)

4 ounces green cabbage, roughly chopped (about $1^3/4$–$2^1/4$ cups)

1 tablespoon fish sauce

1 tablespoon light soy sauce

1 teaspoon sugar

2 tablespoons lime juice

2 small fresh red chilies, finely chopped

2 scallions, finely chopped

2 tablespoons ground roasted peanuts

Bring a pot of water to a boil, add the noodles, and simmer until they soften and separate. Remove, drain, and hold under cold running water to stop the cooking process. Drain well again and set aside.

Place the calamari in a pan, cover with water, and bring to a boil. Using a slotted spoon, scoop out the calamari, drain, and set aside. Dip the cabbage quickly into the boiling water, drain, and set aside.

Place the noodles, calamari, cabbage, and all the remaining ingredients in a bowl and mix well. Turn out onto a serving plate and serve.

Preparation time: 5 minutes   Cooking time: 5 minutes

spicy pork noodles with lime leaves

pad ki mow

1 tablespoon oil

1 garlic clove, finely chopped

1–2 small fresh red or green chilies, finely chopped

4 ounces lean pork, thinly sliced (about ¹/₂ cup)

1 tablespoon fish sauce

1 tablespoon dark soy sauce

1 teaspoon sugar

2 Kaffir lime leaves, finely chopped

1 medium tomato, chopped

8 ounces (dry weight) soaked sen yai noodles (wide rice sticks), rinsed and separated

1 sprig of cilantro, coarsely chopped, for garnishing

In a wok or frying pan, heat the oil and fry the garlic until golden brown. Add the chilies and stir for a couple of seconds, then add the pork and stir well. One at a time, add the fish sauce, dark soy sauce, sugar, and Kaffir lime leaves, stirring quickly after each addition.

Add the tomato, stir until cooked, and then add the noodles. Stir briefly until cooked through. Turn onto a serving dish and garnish with the cilantro.

Preparation time: 5 minutes   Cooking time: 5 minutes

egg noodles with seafood

ba mee talay

1 nest of fresh or dried ba mee noodles (egg noodles)

2 tablespoons oil

2 garlic cloves, finely chopped

2 ounces raw shrimp, peeled and deveined (about 1/3–1/2 cup)

2 ounces crabmeat (about 1/4–1/3 cup)

2 ounces fresh or canned bamboo shoots, sliced (about 1/3–1/2 cup)

8–10 fresh or canned straw mushrooms, cut in half

1 tablespoon light soy sauce

1 tablespoon dark soy sauce

2 tablespoons fish sauce

Pinch of sugar

1/4 cup vegetable broth

Ground white pepper

1 tablespoon flour, mixed with 2 tablespoons water

1 scallion, coarsely chopped

If using fresh noodles, shake the strands loose and set aside. Bring a pot of water to a boil. Using a coarse-meshed strainer or a sieve, dip the noodles (either fresh or dried) into the boiling water. If fresh, leave only for a few seconds; if dry, leave until the nest separates into individual strands, at which point the noodles should be soft. Drain and set aside.

In a wok or frying pan, heat a tablespoon of the oil and fry half the garlic until golden brown. Add the noodles and stir-fry briefly until darker and no longer wet. Turn onto a serving dish and keep hot.

Quickly heat the remaining tablespoon of oil in the pan and fry the rest of the garlic until golden brown. Add the seafood and stir until cooked through. Add the bamboo shoots and straw mushrooms and stir. Add the light and dark soy sauces, the fish sauce, sugar, broth, and a sprinkling of pepper, stirring briefly after each new addition. Add enough of the flour/water mixture to thicken the sauce slightly and cook for 1–2 minutes. Add the scallion, stir, and scoop onto the noodles. Serve.

Preparation time: 5 minutes   Cooking time: 7 minutes

grilled pork with rice noodles

sen mee moo yang

1 pound pork loin, sliced across the grain into very thin strips
   (about 2 cups)

10 ounces (dry weight) rice noodles (about 1^1/2–2 cups)

2 cups bean sprouts

4 ounces carrots, julienned (about ^{3}/4–1 cup)

4 ounces mooli (white radish), julienned (about ^{3}/4–1 cup)

4 ounces cucumber, julienned (about ^{3}/4–1 cup)

30 basil leaves

For the marinade

1 large garlic clove, finely chopped

1 young lemongrass stalk, finely chopped

1 teaspoon five-spice powder

2 tablespoons fish sauce

1 teaspoon sugar

1 teaspoon sesame oil

For the dressing

1 teaspoon sugar

5 tablespoons hot water

2 tablespoons fish sauce

2 tablespoons vinegar

1 garlic clove, finely chopped

2 small fresh red chilies, finely chopped

In a bowl, mix together the marinade ingredients, stirring well. Add the pork strips, toss to coat thoroughly, and allow to marinate for 30 minutes.

Bring a large pot of water to a boil. Dip the rice noodles in the water for 1 minute. Remove and hold under cold running water to stop the cooking process. Drain again and let cool.

To make the dressing, dissolve the sugar in the hot water and add all the remaining ingredients. Stir well and set aside.

Arrange the rice noodles and all the vegetables and basil leaves in a bowl and set aside.

Preheat a barbecue or grill pan until it is very hot. Cook the pork slices for 3 seconds only on each side, then place on a warmed serving dish.

Pour the dressing over the noodles, toss well, and serve with the pork.

Marinating time: 30 minutes   Cooking time: 5 minutes

ground pork noodles with curry powder
gueyteow moo sap

Lettuce, roughly torn

2 tablespoons oil

8 ounces (dry weight) sen yai noodles (wide rice sticks), rinsed for 20 minutes and separated (about 1¼–1½ cups)

1 tablespoon dark soy sauce

1 garlic clove, finely chopped

4 ounces ground lean pork (about ½ cup)

1 tablespoon tang chi (preserved radish)

½ cup broth, plus extra if needed

1 teaspoon curry powder

1 small onion, finely sliced

1 tablespoon fish sauce

1 tablespoon all-purpose flour, mixed with a little water to a thin paste

2 small scallions, finely chopped

Line a serving dish with the lettuce.

Heat half the oil in a wok or frying pan. Add the noodles, stir quickly, and add ½ teaspoon of the dark soy sauce. Stir for 30–60 seconds to prevent sticking. Turn onto the prepared serving dish.

Heat the remaining oil and fry the garlic until golden brown, add the pork, and stir quickly until the meat is lightly cooked. Add the rest of the ingredients one at a time, including the remaining soy sauce, stirring briefly after each addition. The flour/water paste will thicken the sauce; add only a teaspoon at a time. Add more broth if the mixture becomes too dry. Turn the pork mixture onto the noodles and serve.

Preparation time: 5 minutes   Cooking time: 5 minutes

spicy noodles with pork and shrimp
guey teow yum

4 lettuce leaves

4 ounces (soaked weight) sen yai noodles (wide rice sticks), rinsed and separated (about ⅔–¾ cup)

3 ounces pork, finely sliced (about ⅓ cup)

3 ounces raw shrimp, peeled and deveined (about ¾ cup)

1 garlic clove, finely chopped

2 small fresh red chilies, finely chopped

1 tablespoon fish sauce

1 tablespoon lime juice

1 teaspoon sugar

3 ounces celery, finely sliced (about ¾–1 cup)

1 tablespoon ground roasted peanuts

Arrange the lettuce leaves on a serving dish and set aside.

In a pot of boiling water, blanch the noodles for a few seconds. Strain (reserving the water) and tip into a bowl. Cook the pork and shrimp in the reserved water until both are cooked, then scoop out and put in the bowl.

Add all the remaining ingredients to the bowl, stirring well. Spoon onto the lettuce-lined serving dish and serve.

Preparation time: 5 minutes   Cooking time: 5 minutes

beef curry noodles

gueyteow kaek

2 ounces (dry weight) sen lek noodles (rice sticks), soaked in cold
   water for 15 minutes and drained

4 ounces beef, cut into small cubes (about ½ cup)

1 hard-boiled egg

3 tablespoons oil

2 ounces fried tofu, finely sliced (about ½ cup)

1 shallot, finely sliced

1 garlic clove, finely chopped

2 teaspoons red curry paste (see page 72)

¼ cup coconut milk

1 teaspoon curry powder

2 tablespoons fish sauce

1 teaspoon sugar

1 tablespoon ground roasted peanuts

Cilantro leaves, for garnishing

Set the noodles aside, but have a pot of hot water ready in which to warm them. Put the beef in a small pan and cover with water; boil gently for 5–10 minutes. Shell the egg, cut into quarters, and set aside.

Heat 1 tablespoon of oil and fry the sliced tofu until slightly crisp; drain and set aside. Reheat the oil (add a little more if necessary) and fry the shallot until dark golden brown and crisp. Set aside in the pan.

In a separate wok or frying pan, heat the remaining 2 tablespoons of oil, add the garlic, and fry for a few seconds until golden brown. Add the curry paste, stir to mix, and cook for a few seconds. Add the coconut milk, stir thoroughly to blend, and heat through for a few seconds.

With a slotted spoon or strainer, remove the beef from its pan (reserve the cooking water) and add the meat to the mixture in the wok. Stir to make sure each piece of meat is covered with the curry. Add 2 cups of the water in which the beef was boiled (make up the amount with cold water if necessary), along with the curry powder, fish sauce, and sugar. Stir to mix and cook together for about 5 minutes.

Have two serving bowls ready. Bring the pot of hot water for the noodles to a boil, put the noodles in a sieve or strainer with a handle, and dip into the water for a few seconds to warm through. Drain and divide between the serving bowls. Arrange the quartered egg on top of the noodles. Add the peanuts to the beef curry, stir, and pour the curry over the noodles. Garnish with the reserved fried tofu, the fried shallots with a little of their oil, and the cilantro.

Preparation time: 10 minutes   Cooking time: 10 minutes

spicy pork and vermicelli noodle soup
wun sen tom yum

1 tablespoon oil

1 garlic clove, finely chopped

1¼ cups chicken broth

1 teaspoon tang chi (preserved radish)

4 ounces pork, finely sliced (about ½ cup)

3 ounces wun sen noodles (cellophane noodles), soaked for 20 minutes and drained

½ cup bean sprouts

2 tablespoons fish sauce

1 teaspoon sugar

1 tablespoon lime juice

½ teaspoon chili powder

2 teaspoons ground roasted peanuts

1 scallion, finely chopped

In a small pan, heat the oil and fry the garlic until golden brown. Remove from the heat and set aside.

In a saucepan, heat the broth and tang chi. When it is simmering, add the pork slices and all the other ingredients except the garlic oil. When the soup comes to a boil, it is ready to serve: ladle into soup bowls and sprinkle a little of the garlic oil on top.

Preparation time: 3 minutes   Cooking time: 5 minutes

chicken noodles with basil leaves
lahd nah

2 tablespoons oil

8 ounces (dry weight) sen mee noodles (rice vermicelli), soaked in water for 20 minutes and drained (about 1¼–1½ cups)

2 tablespoons light soy sauce

2 garlic cloves, finely chopped

2 fresh red chilies, finely sliced

4 ounces skinless boneless chicken breast, finely sliced (about ½ cup)

20 basil leaves

1 tablespoon fish sauce

¼ cup broth or water, plus extra if needed

1 teaspoon all-purpose flour, mixed with 3 tablespoons water

2 ounces snow peas (about ½ cup)

2 ounces carrots, julienned (about ⅓–½ cup)

1 teaspoon sugar

In a wok or frying pan, heat 1 tablespoon of the oil. Add the noodles, stir quickly, then add 1 tablespoon of the light soy sauce and stir well for 30–60 seconds to prevent sticking. Turn onto a serving dish.

Add the remaining oil to the wok, heat it, then fry the garlic and chilies until the garlic is golden brown. Add the chicken, stir, and cook briefly. Add the basil leaves, fish sauce, and the remaining soy sauce and stir. Add a little broth or water and stir. Add the flour and water mixture and stir in thoroughly. Stir in the vegetables and sugar. Cook for a few seconds until the chicken is cooked through, stirring constantly. Add a little more broth if necessary. Stir, then turn onto the noodles and serve.

Preparation time: 5 minutes   Cooking time: 8 minutes

fried chicken noodles with curry paste
ba mee pad prik gaeng

2 tablespoons oil

2 small garlic cloves, finely chopped

1 tablespoon red curry paste (see page 72)

6 ounces skinless boneless chicken breast, roughly chopped
   (about $3/4$ cup)

1 nest of ba mee noodles (egg noodles), soaked if dried

1 tablespoon dark soy sauce

1 tablespoon light soy sauce

1 teaspoon sugar

1 cup bean sprouts

2 ounces broccoli, cut into small florets (about $1/3$–$1/2$ cup)

2 ounces carrots, julienned (about $1/3$–$1/2$ cup)

Cilantro leaves, for garnishing

In a wok or large frying pan, heat the oil and fry the garlic until golden brown. Add the curry paste and stir well. Next, add all the remaining ingredients one at a time, except the cilantro, stirring once between each addition.

Mix well, turn out onto a serving dish, and garnish with the cilantro.

Preparation time: 3 minutes   Cooking time: 5 minutes

stir-fried noodles with beef and dried chili
gueyteow pad nua

2 tablespoons oil

2 garlic cloves, finely chopped

1 teaspoon finely chopped fresh ginger

1 large dried red chili, coarsely chopped

8 ounces lean beef, thinly sliced (about 1 cup)

1 egg

1 medium onion, finely chopped

1 tablespoon fish sauce

1 tablespoon light soy sauce

1 teaspoon sugar

8 ounces (dry weight) medium flat white flour noodles,
   soaked for 20–30 minutes and drained

4 ounces celery, coarsely chopped (about 1 cup)

Heat the oil in wok or frying pan and fry the garlic until golden brown. Add the ginger and stir, add the chili and stir, then add the beef and stir until it is just cooked through.

Break the egg into the mixture and stir quickly. Add the onion and stir. Add the fish sauce, light soy sauce, and sugar, stirring once. Add the noodles and stir well for a minute. Add the celery, stir briefly, turn onto a plate, and serve.

Preparation time: 5 minutes   Cooking time: 5 minutes

fruits, desserts & drinks

festivals

Festivals are an essential part of Thai life. For Thai people, the primary purpose of celebrating festivals is to have fun, but the festivals also maintain an important link with the traditions and culture of the past. This is especially true in the rural areas where the year is still dictated by the agricultural cycle, so times of toil are punctuated by seasonal festivals that serve as both holidays and propitious occasions. Many festivals follow the lunar calendar and are thus literally movable feasts, while others have set annual dates. However, Thai people certainly have many festivals to celebrate throughout the year, whether religious or secular, royal or political.

Perhaps the most important, best-known, and greatest of Thailand's festivals is Songkran. Songkran is the celebration of the traditional Thai new year, which starts on April 13 and lasts for three days. *Songkran* is a Thai word that means "move" or "change place," as it is the day when the sun changes its position in the zodiac. It is also known as the "Water Festival," as people believe that water will wash away bad luck. The tradition of Songkran is respected by all Thai people irrespective of their status or religion. It is also a family get-together where the younger members pay respects to their elders by pouring scented water onto the hands of their parents and grandparents and presenting them with gifts. They dedicate the merits of this action to their ancestors, and in turn, the elders wish the youngsters good luck and prosperity.

Another popular festival is Loy Krathong, which is celebrated annually on the full moon day of November, the twelfth lunar month. It takes place at a time when the weather is fine, the rainy season is over, and there is a high water level all over the country. On this night, everybody goes to rivers and other waterways to float a *krathong*. Traditionally a krathong is bowl-shaped and made out of banana leaves, with a lotus flower placed in the middle with a lighted candle in its center. The purpose of floating the krathong is, first, to pay homage to the Lord Buddha and the spirits of the water on which the agricultural society depends for its prosperity, and, second, to release trouble and bad luck, which is symbolically carried away on the water.

The Fruit Fair (right and previous pages) is an annual event, usually held during the middle of May, to celebrate the abundance of local fruits and produce. As well as the stalls that sell local fruits and produce, there are colorful floats decorated with fruits, parades and musical and dance processions, beauty pageants, fruit competitions, and exhibitions of local produce.

thai fruits, desserts & drinks
kong-wan, kanom, krueng-deum

Thai desserts and sweets are almost a separate cuisine in themselves. As much care, skill, and artistry goes into their creation as that applied in the best European patisseries. In Thailand, fresh fruit is the normal finale to a meal; sweet desserts are reserved for special occasions and formal entertaining, mainly because they require a lot of preparation and cooking time. Consequently, I have not included recipes for them here but have concentrated on Thai fruits, desserts, and drinks that can be prepared quickly and easily.

Thailand is popularly known as the "land of smiles," but it should be just as well known as a country blessed with a myriad of delicious tropical and temperate fruits. It is a paradise for those who love fruit. Generally, Thai fruits are sweet, but there are some that are sour, like tamarind. The major fruit-producing areas are located mostly in the eastern and southern regions of the country, but the central region also produces a variety of fruit for the markets in every season.

Thailand is never without fruit. In the countryside, some fruit trees, such as banana trees, double as fences around properties. Although they make a much less impenetrable barrier than barbed wire, they provide greenery and fresh air to all living nearby.

durian
du-rian

The durian, considered the "king of fruits" by Thais, is Thailand's most expensive fruit. It looks like a football, ranges from six to ten inches long, and can weigh up to ten pounds. The rind is covered with very sharp spines and the fruit is therefore carried by the stem or on an attached string to avoid damage to the hands. Durian is a distinctive and unusual-tasting fruit. Inside are five sections containing one to several seeds encased within a cream or yellow aromatic, custardlike pulp. The flavor is intriguing and difficult to describe—a custard with almonds, onion, and cream cheese might give some idea of this wonderful fruit. People either love it or hate it. It has a very strong aroma, so strong, in fact, that it is banned from airline cabins, hotels, and some public transportation.

Durian is referred to as a "heating" fruit because it causes the body to feel warm. Overconsumption is said to be balanced by eating a "cooling" fruit like the mangosteen. A commonly held belief is that drinking alcoholic beverages after eating durian can cause illness or death, but this is just a myth.

durian with coconut
sweet sticky rice
nam grati durian

For the coconut sweet sticky rice

1/2 cup coconut milk

1/2 teaspoon salt

1/4 cup sugar

1 3/4 cups freshly coated sticky rice (see page 107)

For the durian mixture

1 cup coconut milk

1/2 teaspoon salt

1/3 cup sugar

1 ripe durian, peeled, pitted, and cut into pieces

Prepare the sticky rice according to the instructions on page 107. Then, to make the coconut sweet sticky rice, mix the ½ cup of coconut milk with the salt and sugar in a bowl until the sugar has dissolved. Stir in the still-warm sticky rice and set aside.

To prepare the fruit mixture, heat the 1 cup of coconut milk with the salt and sugar until the sugar dissolves. Remove from the heat and let cool. Place the durian pieces in the cooled mixture and let them soak briefly.

Arrange the durian on a serving dish beside the sweet sticky rice and serve.

Preparation time: 5 minutes   Cooking time: 30 minutes

mangosteen
mang-kut

The mangosteen is my all-time favorite fruit. Not well known outside Thailand, it is about two inches in diameter and has a thick, purple-black, woody skin. Inside are segments (similar to those of an orange) of sweet, juicy, white flesh. The taste is very refreshing, being both sweet and tart, and the pulp melts onto your tongue. Almost everyone likes mangosteen the first time they try it, and many feel it is the finest fruit in the world. Unfortunately, it is very hard to grow, and also bruises very easily while being transported; the consequent wastage tends to make it expensive.

mango
ma-muang

One of the great fruits of Thailand with a special reputation all its own, the mango comes in several different varieties, used in different ways. It can be eaten unripe, almost white, when it is very crunchy and sour. This is a great favorite in Thailand. It is sliced and eaten with chili dips, a combination that caters perfectly to the Thai love of crunchy texture with sharp, sour tastes. Dessert mangoes have a juicy, orange flesh and can be sliced and eaten on their own, another great favorite. Many feel the best way to enjoy mangoes is with sticky rice and coconut milk—a popular Thai dessert. Mangoes can also be used in ice cream and sorbet.

mango sorbet
ma-muang sobey

1 pound ripe mango, peeled, pitted, and chopped
2/3 cup sugar, dissolved in 1 cup water to make a syrup

Blend the mango with the cooled syrup in a blender or food processor until the mixture is smooth. Put into the freezer in a suitable container for about an hour, until the mixture is slushy and frozen around the edges. Remove and reblend, then return it to the freezer for about 30 minutes. Serve the sorbet with fresh fruit.

Preparation time: 15 minutes   Freezing time: 1 hour 30 minutes

papaya
ma-la-kaw

The delicious papaya is available most of the year, but is at its best during the hot season, from March to July. Oval in shape, the fruit is cut lengthwise to remove the small black seeds in the middle. As with the mango, the papaya is used both unripe and ripe. The best-known use, when the fruit is a very pale beige, is in *Som Tam* (see page 46), for which it is grated, but it can also be used as a vegetable and cooked, generally in curries. When the fruit is ripe, the soft, dark-orange flesh is full of flavor and can be eaten raw with a sprinkling of lime juice to contrast with its sweetness. Combining papaya in a fruit salad with pineapple or a melon such as cantaloupe is delectable.

banana
kluay

Americans are generally familiar with only one type of banana imported there. In Thailand we have many different types growing in abundance. Not only the fruit is used; the leaves make an excellent platter, plate decoration, or wrapper for all kinds of food. Thai bananas range in size from the small lady finger banana to larger types, the tastes and textures also varying widely. The most famous type is *Kluay Hom,* a large specimen with a thick, golden skin. Unripe bananas are sliced and dried in the sun and fried or grilled for a snack. Ripe bananas are sweet and fragrant and nice for eating fresh. Unripe bananas are also preserved in sugar or used in baking. Popular Thai banana dishes are *Kluay Ping* (grilled and soaked with syrup), *Kluay Buat Chi* (boiled in coconut milk), *Kluay Chuiam* (cooked in syrup), *Kluay Phao* (smoked in the skin), and *Kluay Khaek* (golden fritters). Bananas can also form the basis for a good milk shake, and can be dipped in batter (made with rice flour and coconut milk) and deep-fried.

bananas cooked in syrup
kluay chuiam

1 cup sugar
1 cup water
4 large bananas
1/2 cup coconut milk, mixed with 1/4 teaspoon salt,
  for serving (optional)

In a small saucepan, dissolve the sugar in the water. Strain through cheesecloth into a large pan. Peel the bananas and chop into 2-inch pieces. Add to the sugar mixture and bring to a boil. Reduce the heat and cook gently, removing any film that forms on the surface, until the bananas are bright and clear and the sugar syrup forms threads when lifted with a wooden spoon. Serve hot as it is or with the coconut milk mixed with salt to balance the sweetness.

Preparation time: 3 minutes   Cooking time: 30 minutes

coconut
ma-prow

The coconut palm is one of the most versatile of trees, the fruit used in many ways, the leaves for roofs and screens, the sap to make coconut sugar, and the wood itself to make houses. The young coconut, with either a green or yellow exterior, is full of water (not milk), which is sweet, refreshing, and very healthy—a perfect drink. No matter where a coconut grows, the water inside the nut is pure and safe. Vendors selling drinking nuts will open them for you and even give you a straw. After the water has been consumed, the shell is broken open and the immature, jellylike flesh is scraped out with a spoon and eaten. Alternatively, the pulp can be mixed with water, then squeezed to make coconut milk, which is used in many dishes. The flesh of the mature coconut is grated and used in cakes and desserts, including ice cream.

coconut ice cream
ice cream grati

1 cup coconut milk
³/4 cup whipping cream
¹/4 cup sugar
3 tablespoons finely chopped young coconut flesh, or 2 tablespoons
  unsweetened dried coconut, toasted
2 eggs

In a saucepan, combine the coconut milk, whipping cream, sugar, and coconut flesh or dried coconut and bring to a boil. Beat the eggs in a bowl, then whisk the boiling coconut milk mixture into the eggs. Let it cool.

Pour the mixture into a small loaf pan, cover it, and freeze until firm. Break up the ice cream, then tip it into a bowl and beat with an electric beater or in a food processor until smooth. Spoon the mixture back into the pan, cover, and freeze for several hours until firm.

Preparation time: 10 minutes   Freezing time: 3 hours

squash in coconut milk
gaeng buad fak tong

1 cup coconut milk
8 ounces squash, peeled and cut into 1-inch cubes
¹/4 cup sugar

In a pan, bring the coconut milk to a boil, add the squash and sugar, and simmer until the squash is soft. When ready, turn onto a serving dish.

Preparation time: 5 minutes   Cooking time: 5 minutes

rambutan
ngoh

The name of this fruit is derived from the Malay word *rambut*, meaning "hair." This is because the fruit's rind is covered with red and yellow spikes. Thai rambutans, grown mostly in the south and east, are sweet and succulent, the juicy flesh coming easily away from the pit. Favorite varieties are *Ngoh Rong Rien* and *Ngoh Si Chompoo*. Thais are experts at delicately carving away the sweet flesh from the central stone.

rambutan in syrup
ngoh loy geow

1 cup sugar
2 cups water
8 rambutans, peeled and pitted
Crushed ice, for serving

In a small saucepan, bring the sugar and water gently to a boil, stirring occasionally. Boil for 10 minutes, until a thin syrup has formed. Put the rambutans in a bowl, pour the syrup over them, and stir well. Serve with ice to make them really cold.

Preparation time: 5 minutes   Cooking time: 12 minutes

longan
lam-yai

The longan is one of northern Thailand's most succulent fruits. You will see longans, or "dragon's eyes," in Chiangmai's supermarkets—clusters of small, brown fruit (about the size of a large grape) still attached to a bouquet of thin branches and green leaves. This is the best way to eat them, straight from the branch as nature intended. The outer shell is very thin and readily peels away to reveal the moist, juicy interior. The flesh, not unlike that of a lychee, surrounds a shiny brown seed and is opalescent with a delicate flavor, giving a good balance between sweetness and acidity.

The Thai longan is known as one of the best in the world, the sweet, pinkish-white flesh believed by many to energize the body and banish fatigue. Longans can be enjoyed as a dessert with either sugar syrup or sticky rice.

sago and longan in coconut milk
lamyai saku peeak

2¹/₂ cups water
2 ounces sago (about ¹/₃ cup)
1 cup sugar
4 ounces longans, pitted (about 1 cup)
¹/₂ cup coconut milk, mixed with ¹/₂ teaspoon salt, for serving

In a large pan, bring the water to a boil, add the sago, and cook until it swells. Add the sugar and longans and cook briefly.

Spoon into serving bowls and cover with the coconut milk. Add salt to the mixture to taste.

Preparation time: 5 minutes   Cooking time: 5 minutes

guava
farang

The guava is a well-known fruit that is plentiful in Thailand, although it originated in Spain. Thai people call it *farang*, the same name they use for Westerners. A great snack, guavas can be eaten either ripe or when still green, dipped in a little salt or sugar. They also taste great when conserved and are the basis of luscious, highly refreshing drinks. There are many kinds of guavas; when peeled, they reveal white, bright red, or pink flesh. The white-fleshed variety is widely available in Thailand and is the most popular.

pummelo
som-o

A member of the citrus family, the pummelo is similar to a grapefruit, although its sections can be peeled apart more easily. The flesh is succulent, with a delicious sour-sweet flavor. The finest Thai pummelos are those from the central region, especially from Nakhon Pathom, Chai Nat, and Phichit. Sweet and tangy, pummelos can be enjoyed in a salad or on their own with sugar syrup.

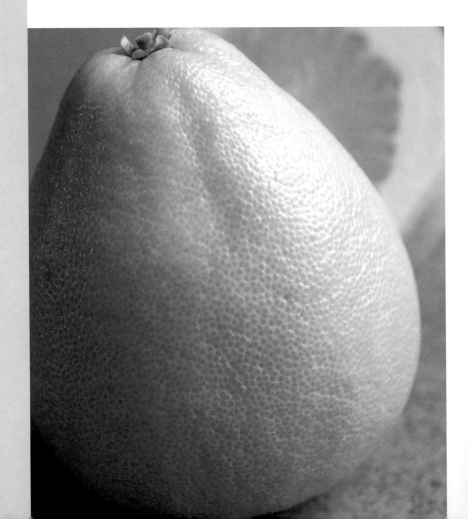

pineapple
sapparot

Thailand is one of the largest producers of this flavorful, juicy fruit, which is best grown in sandy coastal soil. The pineapple grows year-round, not on a tree as might be expected, but on a low plant. Pineapple is a versatile fruit that can be used for desserts, drinks, and savory dishes.

pineapple conserve
sapparot guan

In Thailand, we use brass pans for cooking fruit with sugar, but you could use one made from good-quality stainless steel. This conserve will keep for one month, and is delicious served with ice cream.

1 cup sugar
1 pineapple (about 2^{1}/4 pounds), peeled, cored, and finely chopped

In a saucepan, dissolve the sugar in 1 cup of water over gentle heat and add the pineapple. Mix thoroughly and stir over medium heat until the mixture forms a soft ball, then allow it to cool.

Preparation time: 10 minutes   Cooking time: 30 minutes

rose apple
chom-poo

Similar in shape to a pear, the rose apple has a glossy skin that is either green or pink in color. It has a crisp, crunchy texture and an extremely refreshing taste. Thais like to eat it dipped in salt, sugar, and chilies.

thai fruit salad
frut sa-lad

4 rose apples, cut in half, pitted, and cut into small cubes
1 ripe mango, peeled, pitted, and cut into small cubes
1 small ripe papaya, peeled, seeded, and cut into small cubes
1/2 pummelo, peeled, rind removed, segments broken apart and cut
  again into small pieces
1/2 pineapple, peeled, cored, and cubed
1 tablespoon finely chopped fresh ginger
1 tablespoon lemon juice
1 tablespoon sugar
10 mint leaves, finely chopped

Arrange the fruit in a bowl. Add the ginger, lemon juice, sugar, and chopped mint leaves. Mix well and chill in the refrigerator before serving.

Preparation time: 10 minutes

watermelon
taeng-mo

The most common watermelon in Thailand is pink-fleshed. The melon is simply cut and sliced lengthwise and served plain. The taste is mild but sweet and refreshing. It makes a fabulous drink when blended with ice. The seeds are toasted and eaten as a snack.

watermelon quench
nam taeng-mo pun

2 tablespoons sugar
1/4 cup water
1 ripe watermelon, peeled
Pinch of salt

In a small pan, gently heat the sugar and water until the sugar dissolves. Let it cool.

Cut the watermelon into small pieces, removing the seeds and rind. Put some of the pieces into a blender with some ice cubes, the sugar syrup, and a pinch of salt to taste. Blend, pour into glasses, and serve.

Preparation time: 5 minutes

tropical fruit drinks
nam-pun

There are many different types of fruit juices enjoyed in Thailand and they are all great thirst-quenchers, especially during the hot months between March and July. A great variety of fruits is used in drinks, including bananas, guavas, papayas, oranges, pineapples, watermelons, coconuts, longans, and mangoes.

tea
nam cha

Cha Ron *Hot Tea*
Cha Yen *Iced Tea with Milk*
Cha Dam Yen *Iced Tea without Milk*

In Thailand, tea is grown in the north, in hilly areas where the climate is cooler. Sometimes we enjoy our tea hot in the traditional Chinese manner. For iced tea with milk, we make the tea stronger, add sugar and sweetened condensed milk, and serve it in a glass with plenty of ice. For iced tea without milk, we add more sugar, stir well, let it cool to room temperature, then pour it over a full glass of ice and garnish with lime slices.

lemongrass tea
nam takrai

5 cups water
2 lemongrass stalks, rinsed and lightly crushed, or 2 ounces ginger,
* cut into 1-inch pieces and roughly sliced (about 1/4 cup)*
Sugar, to taste

In a saucepan, heat the water. When it begins to boil, add the crushed lemongrass or ginger, cover, and continue to boil for 5 minutes.

Pour the contents of the pan into a teapot. Add sugar to taste and serve as hot tea.

coffee
ka fee

I love to have iced coffee with my lunch and as an afternoon drink. In Thailand, we prepare our coffee with condensed milk or sugar syrup instead of fresh milk.

Ka Fee Yen *Iced Coffee with Milk*
Make some strong black coffee, add sugar and sweetened condensed milk, and stir well. Let it cool to room temperature, then pour it over a full glass of ice and top with unsweetened condensed milk.

Oliang *Sweetened Iced Black Coffee*
Make some strong black coffee. Fill a glass with ice shavings and add the coffee, sweetening to taste with a simple sugar syrup.

Ka Fee Dam *Black Coffee*
A cup of good, strong, brewed or percolated coffee.

Ka Fee Ron *Hot Coffee with Milk*
As this coffee is served without sugar, we use canned, unsweetened, evaporated milk.

Ka Fee Dam Ron *Black Coffee with Sugar*
Sugar syrup is added to strong black coffee.

index